Just wanted to thank you so much for your in-depth and thoughtful articles regarding housing our community! They were spot on and shed light on such an important topic. Thank you for your hard work in covering the topic and for getting the word out about our organization and the work we are doing!

April Long,
PROGRAM DIRECTOR | WEST MOUNTAIN REGIONAL HOUSING COALITION

I wanted to write and express my gratitude to you both and Aspen Journalism for your excellent series on the challenges in our communities and in particular, housing for our workforce. I am honored that you took the time to travel throughout the region and visit our projects, in addition to listening to my concerns and vision for creating decent homes for the families and individuals serving our local institutions and economy. I appreciated Habitat RFV having been included in the articles, alongside work being done by so many others. You created a comprehensive perspective on the unaddressed basic needs of the communities, provided clarity on the changes that have taken place in these sleepy little mountain towns, and defined the concerning trajectory we are on.

Gail Schwartz,
PRESIDENT | HABITAT FOR HUMANITY ROARING FORK

Your multipart Aspen Journalism series on facets of community in our valley, hit a home run this New Year's weekend as volunteers created a lovely sit-down Christmas dinner at the Aspen Chapel, so well chronicled for all of us to enjoy in your story.

Tim McFlynn | ASPEN JOURNALISM BOARD MEMBER

In a world of technology, artificial intelligence,
and internet domination,
Paul looks right into the heart of real people.
The primordial aspect of our existence functions
around community and a sense of place.
He helps us take a moment to change our focus, and
look at the real people and communities
that make a positive impact every day.

Sean Strode | MAYOR, RIFLE, COLORADO

'It takes a village' is the often-used cliché about raising children, but
to build something in one place that lasts,
it definitely 'takes a community'.
The concept of 'neighbor-hood' is really the foundation
of such local communities.
People, neighbors, looking out foreach other in their local 'hood'.
It is as simple as that. By defining this in such specific terms
Paul Andersen has written a manual of how to put this into action.
An invaluable primer for all local organizers.

Nicholas Vesey | MINISTER, ASPEN CHAPEL

Community residents experience, but few are fully aware,
that community strength and cohesion are the foundation
upon which community success is built.
Cohesion and strength do not arise effortlessly.
Instead, they require understanding then action by residents.
Much of that understanding requires factual, thorough,
and even entertaining storytelling.
Paul Andersen has a long history of delivering
those kinds of stories to communities.

Michael Kinsley,
FORMER COMMUNITY ACTIVIST AND COUNTY COMMISSIONER,
RETIRED DIRECTOR OF SUSTAINABLE COMMUNITIES
AT ROCKY MOUNTAIN INSTITUTE

I am writing to thank you for your excellent series on
Community in our western Colorado valleys.
You provided a clear view of the social structure
which governs our communities and economies.
This introspective look will prove invaluable to elected officials
and anyone interested in improving life in western Colorado.
My wife and I have lived here for 51 years,
and your accounts ring true.
The intercommunity dynamics are fascinating and
will be interesting to readers here and statewide.
We are pleased to hear that these valuable insights
will be available in book form.

Bill Kane | MAYOR, BASALT, COLORADO

Today's article is fantastic. Off the charts.
Incredibly accurate and thorough. You really nailed it.
Thank you on behalf of all the housing advocates in the region.

David Myler,
DIRECTOR WEST MOUNTAIN REGIONAL
HOUSING AUTHORITY

Paul's series offers essential perspectives on the importance
of considering the role each of us plays in creating a community
and the interconnected nature of our incredible region.

Allison Alexander,
DIRECTOR, STRATEGIC PARTNERSHIPS
AND COMMUNICATION,
ASPEN COMMUNITY FOUNDATION

BOOKS BY PAUL ANDERSEN

Elevations

The Town that Said 'Hell, No!'

The Friends' Hut

High Road to Aspen

The Story of Snowmass

Moonlight Over Pearl

Aspen | Rocky Mountain Paradise

Aspen's Rugged Splendor

Power in the Mountains

East of Aspen

Aspen | Body, Mind, & Spirit

Elk Mountains Odyssey

The Preacher and the Pilot

Aspen | Portrait of a Rocky Mountain Town

Aspen in Color

IN SEARCH OF
COMMUNITY

Traffic jams on Highway 82 at Willits reveal the commuter culture of the Roaring Fork Valley and beyond.
DANIEL BAYER/ASPEN JOURNALISM

In Search of Community

FROM ASPEN TO PARACHUTE

*Lavish second homes, short-term rentals,
soaring housing costs,
and a workforce of long-distance commuters
necessitate a reexamination of community
in a regional context.*

PAUL ANDERSEN

ASPEN JOURNALISM | ASPEN, COLORADO

In Search of Community
Copyright © 2024 by Paul Andersen

DESIGN | Curt Carpenter

ISBN | 979-8-9892335-3-3

All rights reserved. No part of this book may be reproduced or transmitted in any form or by any means, electronic or mechanical, including photocopying, recording, or by any information storage and retrieval system, without permission in writing from the publisher.

Made possible through a generous grant from the Aspen Business Center Foundation.

PRINTED IN THE UNITED STATES

Aspen Journalism
local. non profit. investigative.

1280 Ute Avenue, Suite 9 | Aspen, Colorado 81611
www.aspenjournalism.org

TABLE OF CONTENTS

	Introduction	xiii
	Foreword	xvii
CHAPTER 1	Embracing Regionalism	1
CHAPTER 2	Nourishing Community	11
CHAPTER 3	Aspen's Embattled First Communities	19
CHAPTER 4	The "Quiet Years" of Aspen	33
CHAPTER 5	Skiing and Culture Define Aspen's Future	41
CHAPTER 6	Aspen: Community or Commodity?	51
CHAPTER 7	Community Blossoms Along the Colorado River	69
CHAPTER 8	Building Livable Communities	95
CHAPTER 9	The Housing Conundrum	113
CHAPTER 10	Housing Challenges and Solutions	127
	Housing Non-Profit Agencies	149
	About the Author	151

INTRODUCTION

WHY I CARE ABOUT COMMUNITY

I NEVER REALLY UNDERSTOOD COMMUNITY until I found one that touched my heart. Born in Chicago, Illinois, I came west to discover Crested Butte, Colorado, the place where I truly came of age.

The first time I laid eyes on that charming grid of dirt streets in the summer of 1969, I fell in love with a unique place.

In a sense, Crested Butte became my spiritual home, a place that, despite dramatic changes, still kindles something sacred. That attachment grew dramatically in the late-'70s/early '80s when the town rose up as a mostly unified whole to battle a huge international mining conglomerate intent on perpetrating an industrial eyesore by developing an enormous molybdenum mine on Mt. Emmons, beneath Red Lady Bowl, just five miles west of town.

The "Save the Lady" campaign on which I reported as editor of the Crested Butte Chronicle, had every element of "the good fight": a small and spirited community facing off against an economic and industrial juggernaut. After five years of unified resistance and community solidarity during a pitched environmental battle, the mining company withdrew. Crested Butte had prevailed, thanks to a community that summoned hidden resources among its eclectic population that few of us knew existed. The town's greatest strength was a mutual love of place for a small and cohesive community that declared and defended its autonomy in a fundamental display of the democratic principle of self-determination.

In 1984, I rode my mountain bike across the Elk Range for a job interview with the *Aspen Times* where I took on the role of reporter. In Aspen, I discovered a complex community built upon multiple social layers spanning diverse historic epochs. The value of community in Aspen was deep-seated for many locals who strove to protect their special place from the commoditizing influences that have long threatened the higher values defining what many consider the soul of the town.

That struggle continues today and will, long into the future, as the resort workforce is pushed further and further downvalley in what equates to a theme park dynamic: Workers commute upvalley for service industry jobs only to leave at the end of their shifts because they can't afford to live in the community they serve. The economic disparity influencing the housing market results in fracturing the social structure that once gave Aspen the "messy vitality" planning goal touted by Aspen and Pitkin County.

The 10-part Aspen Journalism series on community that I initiated in December 2023, of which this book is a compilation, begins with a focus on regionalism, which seeks to broaden the notion of community along the 80-mile commuter corridor, from Aspen to Parachute. A series within the series then peels back the historic layers of Aspen to reveal the decades-long struggle for community identity that surfaces regularly today in opinion columns and letters-to-the-editor.

The series continues with emergent expressions of community in the Colorado River communities of New Castle, Silt and Rifle—communities that cherish their individual identities and evolving characters while recognizing and relying on regional affiliations. In these dynamic communities, all of which have become homes for displaced Aspenites, I discovered a wider appreciation for social cohesion based on diversity, mutuality and the psycho-emotional need for community in every walk of life.

The final three parts of the series focus on affordable, accessible housing as the keystone to achieving community health and sustainability throughout a region where escalating housing costs intensify a widespread lack of opportunity for working people. The series concludes that affordable, accessible housing is vital to sense of place, community cohesion and the sought after well-being that comes from stability and security, the most fundamental of human needs.

Overarching all is the importance of establishing communities of neighborhoods and neighbors where people work and live, put down roots, and live harmoniously together by forming a mutuality of interests and needs that transcend politics, incomes, race, religion and other social divisions, communities that endeavor to cultivate social diversity and unify during times of need.

—PAUL ANDERSEN
October, 2024

FOREWORD

GREATER ROARING FORK FATES INTERTWINED

THE 10-PART *IN SEARCH OF COMMUNITY* series written by Paul Andersen, initially produced as a reporting project for the nonprofit, investigative news organization Aspen Journalism, was a journey with an inspiration point that came in October 2023 when I joined Paul for a hike up to the base of one the Fryingpan Valley's Seven Castles.

On our agenda as we sat beneath the imposing rock formations a few miles up from Basalt was a chat about following up an event that Paul and Aspen Journalism presented the previous March—a screening of *High Country*, a film about Crested Butte's efforts to preserve the soul of its community. The gathering also included a convening of local leaders before the film and a panel discussion afterward addressing the challenges facing Aspen and the Roaring Fork Valley. We knew we were on to something, based on the enthusiasm among the 75 or so people who turned out to continue engaging in similar events and discussions.

As we gazed down the 'Pan and toward the midvalley below, we talked about what a remarkable slice of earth we inhabit—what a beautiful, spirited, unusual, often troubled, always changing sort of place the Roaring Fork watershed is and how despite the many differences and conflicts that emerge, there is a growing common circumstance uniting those in this urban-yet-rural region between Independence Pass and De Beque Canyon. In this corridor spanning more than 100 miles bridging Aspen and Parachute, we share an attachment to the land and a dependence on our environment and water. We participate in a growing economy where what happens in Aspen has impacts far downstream, just as the choices made by citizens along the Colorado River in Garfield County have consequences for their counterparts in Eagle and Pitkin counties. Ultimately, for anyone with a stake in this "greater Roaring Fork region," our fates are intertwined and we increasingly rely on each other for basic needs. Paul and I decided that the time was right to pursue in-depth reporting that would reexamine what community means in this regional context.

Paul, who has written 15 books about the region and has long been a contributor to local newspapers, including a nearly 40-year run at the *Aspen Times* as an editor, reporter and columnist, took to the project with a drive and dedication I had rarely seen in my 20 years in journalism. We kicked off the series on Dec. 23, co-publishing as we did each article with *Aspen Daily News*, delving into the increasing trends toward regionalism from Aspen to Parachute. The series concluded in June with its final installments examining that mother of all regional challenges—affordable housing. As what was once Aspen's problem becomes the pressing issue everywhere, Paul's reporting looked at how a growing movement is treating the scarcity of affordable housing as a social justice issue and moral imperative to address. Along the way, the series covered the history of what community has meant in the Roaring Fork Valley going back to pre-mining days, how Aspen grew into what it is today and how a new generation of leaders are setting positive intentions for the future of their towns in the Colorado River Valley.

The series struck a chord for framing big questions facing the community in this larger regional context. Paul was able to channel a feeling shared by many as we absorb the changes wrought by the COVID-19 pandemic and their impact on our region—the growth of short-term rentals and second homes reshaping neighborhoods, new waves of migration driving growth and sending housing costs soaring valleywide. Paul interviewed dozens as he traveled up and down the corridor, painting a most comprehensive picture of the state of the community at the beginning of what feels like a new era.

As the series reminds us, community manifests in ever changing ways and the generational question at the heart of Aspen's modern history remains unresolved—where do you draw the line between community and commodity?

It has been an honor and a privilege to publish this work, which we could not have done without a generous grant from the McBride family's Aspen Business Center Foundation that funded the series, as well as printing this book. Our deepest thanks to them, to all the sources who contributed, and to our readers for going on this journey with us. We hope it inspires deeper contemplation of our connections to one another and a sense of purpose to meet the challenges ahead.

—CURTIS WACKERLE
Editor and Executive Director
Aspen Journalism
October, 2024

Interstate 70 follows the Colorado River through a transitional landscape between New Castle and Glenwood Springs. The roadway is a critical part of the infrastructure that connects a community of about 90,000 residents between Aspen and Parachute.

ANDRE SALVAIL/ASPEN DAILY NEWS

CHAPTER I

Embracing Regionalism

"When we try to pick out anything by itself, we find it hitched to everything else in the universe."

—JOHN MUIR

THE COMMUNITY I am searching for extends more than 80 miles, from Aspen to Parachute. This contiguous, linear city clusters along Highway 82 and Interstate 70, and has a population of about 90,000—roughly the size of Longmont—and that's before counting the second homeowners and tourists.

This sprawling community occupies two highway corridors traversing three counties, nine municipalities, at least six additional "census-designated places," four school districts and hundreds of neighborhoods and housing developments composed of vacation properties, single-family homes, condominiums, mobile home parks, apartments, lofts, duplexes and subsidized worker housing.

Geographically, this interdependent community expands with 15 arterial tributary valleys feeding into the main stems of the Roaring Fork and Colorado rivers. It spans from the Continental Divide on Independence Pass in Pitkin County, down the Roaring Fork Valley through Eagle County into western Garfield County, to the mouth of De Beque Canyon. Diverse landscapes include the high alpine to the upper Sonoran life zones, granitic 14,000-foot peaks to desert shales, and numerous ecosystems, from tundra to desert scrub.

The region contains an enormous watershed that feeds the Colorado River, one of the most important river systems in the Western United States, on which six downstream states and a region of northern Mexico depend for water diversions to slake an increasingly insatiable thirst.

This community is contiguous but divided, homogenous but diverse, connected yet fractured. This community is complex and often at odds with itself over its past, its present and especially its future. It contains microcommunities delineated by overlaps and separations, yet strongly influenced socioeconomically by Aspen and Snowmass.

Recognizing regionalism as a social and cultural value that provides strength and cohesion is gradually gaining adherents through a multiplicity of burgeoning social and professional relationships that are striving to transcend parochial differences.

FINDING COMMON GROUND

"THIS REGION IS REALLY ONE COMMUNITY a very mobile workforce," said David Myler, founder of the West Mountain

Downvalley population growth has spawned a regional workforce that serves the upscale resorts of Aspen and Snowmass where an increasing number of luxury and second homes require service and provide employment for commuters who create frequent backups on Highway 82 approaching the city of Aspen.
CONTRIBUTED PHOTO

Regional Housing Coalition, a nonprofit that seeks solutions to affordable housing from Aspen to Parachute. "That workforce is mobile because of Highway 82 and I-70, but we are one community.

Do we have differences? Of course: political differences, economic differences, all kinds of differences. But we're basically one community connected by a workforce that drives up and down the valley every day."

This community is made up of people we see in the grocery stores, at the gas stations, in the post office, on RFTA buses, highways and byways, ski runs, bike rides, wilderness trails, parks, concerts, hot springs pools and many shared public places. Here on our common ground, high in our mountain redoubt, we watch global events unfold while living across a diverse topography with disparate overlays of ethnicity, wealth, poverty, hard work, celebration, recreation, enjoyment and wonder.

Those advancing the notion of a regional community describe the need to unify this far-ranging space. They seek to establish a common thread of understanding in order to collaborate on a collective vision of community cohesion in pursuit of the humane values of dignity, respect, equal opportunity and well-being, all of which must be cultivated, nurtured and appreciated if this overarching community is to achieve a healthy, sustainable future.

"We've seen a shift since 2020 in community engagement," said Evan Zislis, director of the Hurst Initiative at the Aspen Institute.

"We've seen a willingness to reach out across party lines, across county lines, thinking and acting beyond the scope of jurisdictions in order to leverage resources, ideas and expertise. What I've learned is the power of collaboration when it is fueled by a commitment to each other."

David Myler is the founder of the West Mountain Regional Housing Coalition, a nonprofit that seeks solutions to affordable housing from Aspen to Parachute.
PAUL ANDERSEN/ASPEN JOURNALISM

For the past five years, Zislis has formed cohorts of select community leaders, from Aspen to Parachute, who take part in discussion seminars designed to build civic relationships and community outreach.

"It's easy to lose sight of who we are in this place," said Zislis, "and it's easy for us to lose visual sight of each other. We're separated by topography, by rivers and mountains. There is some significant distance between us, so it's easy for us to forget who we are until we just point out the obvious: that we share a workforce. All of these folks, in whatever industry they're in—hospitality and tourism or outdoor recreation or construction—they all live and work in this region."

Zislis and the Hurst Initiative cohorts affirm that regionalism must become a strength within a distended yet interdependent social network.

"Evan believes, as do I, that regional collaborative dialogue is the best way to find solutions for the challenges of the day," Jeff Layman, town administrator of Silt, wrote in an endorsement on the program's website. "To this end, he has worked to bring a diverse collection of

Evan Zislis leads the Hurst Community Initiative, a program of the Aspen Institute dedicated to building civic partnerships among leaders from Aspen to Parachute.
CONTRIBUTED PHOTO

folks together on multiple fronts to increase understanding and work cooperatively."

"Part of this initiative," said Zislis, "is getting people to remember that these are all stakeholders who are integral to the community—doctors, nurses, mental health professionals— these are folks who live throughout this continuum of geography from Aspen to Parachute. We could not survive without each other."

A regional perspective, he said, is about improving the quality of life for the people who live and work here.

LIVE LOCALLY, CARE GLOBALLY

NURTURING CONNECTIVITY through regional relationships is important when considering population trends. The 2020 census showed slow growth around Pitkin County's resort centers with increasing rates of unoccupied homes, happening in concert with what could be described as explosive population growth in the region's last remaining bastions of affordability, in the Colorado River Valley between Silt and Battlement Mesa. Parachute and Battlement Mesa were among the Western Slope towns that saw the largest population increases in the last census, with Parachute up 28.1% and Battlement Mesa up 21.6%.

This population growth is driven in large part by Latinos, who make up around 27% of the Aspen to Parachute population, with numbers concentrated downvalley. Garfield County's Latino population increased 22% in the census.

In Pitkin County, the population rose only 1.2% between 2010 and 2020, according to the census. Meanwhile, the rate of unoccupied homes increased. In Aspen, the share of unoccupied homes rose from 40.7% to 42.9% of the housing stock, according to the census. This helps explain a vast number of nonresidents who move through the

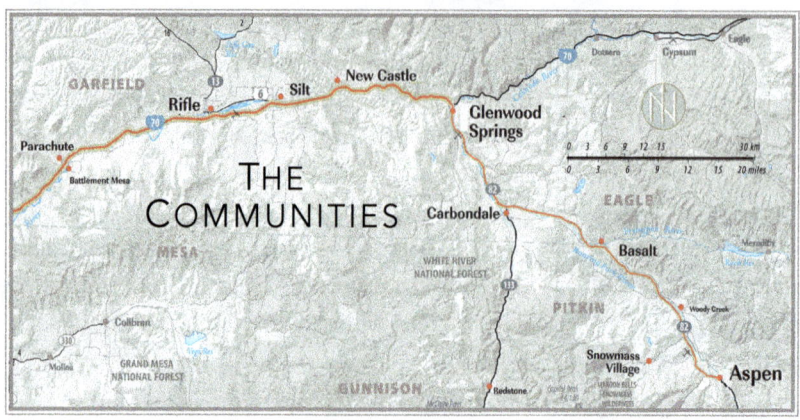

The 80-mile long Aspen-to-Parachute corridor
CURT CARPENTER

county on any given day. According to a 2020 analysis commissioned by Pitkin County examining 2019 data, peak population in the county, experienced around the Christmas and Fourth of July holidays, reached more than 53,000. Just under 18,000 were residents, with over 17,000 occupying overnight accommodations, 10,000 part-time residents and 8,200 commuting into the county to work.

The region's growing downvalley workforce migration along with a shrinking stock of local-occupied housing in Aspen has contributed over the years to what many perceive as a diluting of the once-cohesive Aspen community. Demographic data supports the observation and concern shared by many, that a key driver shaping the community is more luxury, oftentimes in vacant homes upvalley requiring increasing services provided by those living downvalley.

In the farthest western reaches, the echo of regionalism as defined by mutuality with Aspen may seem dim. Divergent community values maintain barriers even while socioeconomic linkages have become stronger.

"I don't know that I would define Aspen to Parachute as being one community," said Parachute Town Manager Travis Elliot, "but we're certainly interconnected by a lot of the challenges we face and by the people who go up and down the valley each day on super-commutes. There are a lot of organizations that work together on a lot of projects

Basalt Mayor Bill Kane has lived in both Aspen and Basalt and sees each town in the valley increasingly developing its own sense of culture and independence.
PAUL ANDERSEN/ASPEN JOURNALISM

and initiatives. I can't even count the number of nonprofits that stretch down the valley and help us with community challenges."

Basalt Mayor Bill Kane also acknowledges differences. "Basalt is different from Aspen, and Carbondale is different from both," he said.

"They each have unique qualities, and that's good."

Having lived in both Aspen and Basalt, Kane appreciates cultural diversity and community independence.

"It used to be that living downvalley meant relying on Aspen's culture and entertainment," said Kane. "Now, Basalt has its own culture, and so does Carbondale."

Cultural context is subject to external forces, however, including the arrival in November 2023 of 80 South American migrants who were forced to take shelter in winter conditions under the bridge at Highway 133 and Highway 82, at the edge of Carbondale. This displaced group of Venezuelans seeking succor in the U.S. had made a harrowing journey to Colorado at the onset of winter.

Suddenly, the woes of the world were delivered to our doorstep as a test of our regional community to care for an influx that may be more than any single municipality can manage.

Such emergent global perspectives force us to bear witness to the larger community of mankind in a world torn by upheavals where millions flee for their lives from a rising tide of climate change, war and civil unrest.

Dramatic changes are sweeping across all nations and all peoples, altering the interconnected human fabric that spreads in an overlay across it all. Accommodating, willingly or not, these externalities requires a strong, positive regional identity to avert despair and emotional fatigue. Regionalism could provide the necessary cohesion to live locally and care globally.

NEW CONTEXT FOR CONNECTIVITY

Clark Anderson is the founder and director of Community Builders, a nonprofit that provides vision to communities in crisis. PAUL ANDERSEN/ASPEN JOURNALISM

"WHEN I LOOK AT THIS VALLEY," said Clark Anderson, founder and director of Community Builders, a nonprofit that provides vision to communities in crisis, "my dream would be that we can rethink who really is part of our community with a much more expansive look. We must look beyond what we have today and ask: What if we took a radical re-imagining of what this place would be like if we all worked together to create a valley or region that's connected with neighborhoods, with real people living in them who feel like they're connected to this place, and that we're not just cogs in a machine feeding a set of jobs that are supporting a pretty small part of the 'community'?"

Within that community, at times we bump up against one another begrudgingly, and at other times we encounter one another with pleasure and joy for what we, together, derive from the sense of being in an extraordinary place. As we fuel this high-octane economic engine, it's hard not to feel like a cog, whether building infrastructure or conserving open space, wielding a nail gun or writing a newspaper column, driving a bus or performing surgery, controlling avalanches or administering first aid, teaching children or caring for seniors.

"A regional perspective is especially important for our rural resort community because of where we are located geographically and by our historical context," said Allison Alexander, director of strategic partnerships and communication for the Aspen Community Foundation.

"In the last few years, more of our workforce has been moved farther and farther away from what is considered the center of our economic region. It is important to think about how those community members and their families are cared for, wherever they are in our region. We are at a moment in time where thinking regionally is really critical."

A high-functioning regional community has the resources and wherewithal to orchestrate the energy, vision, contention, love, care, disappoint-

Allison Alexander is the director of strategic partnerships and communication for the Aspen Community Foundation. CONTRIBUTED PHOTO

Former Aspen Mayor John Bennett recalls when the city "was quite a distance mentally, socially and psychologically from the rest of the valley." That has changed, he said. CONTRIBUTED PHOTO

ment, frustration, joy and sorrow of those who live, work and socialize in close proximity and in common purpose toward the pursuit of happiness, a founding promise of the American experience.

"We are growing out of the parochial identities that we had for decades when we were all more isolated," said former Aspen Mayor John Bennett, who recalls when the city "was quite a distance mentally, socially and psychologically from the rest of the valley. There really wasn't a lot of social communication between communities, and that has really changed because people are on the move much more and from farther distances. There is also a growing sense of regional identity that we, as a valley, are all in this together and not in isolated silos anymore."

Mutual self-interest within this region seems to be nurturing a citizenry poised to carry a burden of labor and to make a commitment to creating and improving a cherished place to live, brimming with rewards, challenges and responsibilities, in equal measure.

This extended rural community, aligned along urban highway corridors, is our communal home, a place of unique cultural characteristics where we ideally discover spirit or soul, the intangible spark that many fear is in decline. Be it ever so humble or grand, messy or vital, home is what community is all about.

And the stronger the sense of home, the stronger the people who live here.

"I wanted to invite people who are new to the valley, like seasonal employees who might not have a big kitchen at home where they can make a really big meal and might not have many people to share it with," said Spencer Bernhardt, a ski instructor who inspired the Aspen Chapel Christmas potluck dinner.

PAUL ANDERSEN/ASPEN JOURNALISM

CHAPTER 2

Nourishing Community

Sharing meals builds bridges
and creates welcoming spaces

THERE ARE FEW more-intimate ways of creating social capital than by sharing nourishment. Community potlucks are a long-standing tradition in many communities where dishes are prepared and shared, along with conversation, laughter and love.

"Hosting new friends" was the heading for a holiday celebration Dec. 17, 2024 at the Aspen Chapel, where the congregation embarked on an ambitious plan to serve holiday dinners to 60 guests in a Christmas community potluck.

The list of food items was ambitious as the chapel congregation was asked to bring a variety of dishes. Volunteer crews were organized to set up and take down chairs and tables and decorate the chapel community room with festive accouterments for the holidays.

"This dinner was for lifties, ski instructors and service workers who have come into Aspen from Chile, Argentina, South Africa, Peru and other faraway places," said chapel minister Nicholas Vesey, who led a raucous caroling session after a turkey dinner with all the fixings.

"We wanted to give them a good Christmas."

And so they did. The chapel was festive with white linen tablecloths, white ceramic plates and complete utensils for a stylish sit-down dinner. As the guests arrived, first in a trickle and then in a flood of young people from all over the world, Vesey, attired in a Santa hat, greeted everyone with cheerful welcomes, handshakes and hugs.

Chapel volunteers did the same. Soon the tables were filled as a convivial atmosphere brightened the room. The chapel hosted the dinner, but the idea came from a young congregant, Spencer Bernhardt, who is teaching skiing at Snowmass for his second consecutive season. "Every town or city I've lived in has had a church dinner or church lunch," Bernhardt said with a smile as the festivities grew into a communal celebration.

"I hadn't seen one in Aspen, so I looked around and thought the Aspen Chapel would be the best place to do it," he said. "I attend some of the services here and tune in to others, and I think it's just a great place. Whoever you are, you are welcome to come here. That's the chapel's message."

Bernhardt proposed the idea to Vesey, who readily agreed. "I

Chef Jeff Spiroff served a complete turkey dinner to guests at the Aspen Chapel Christmas potluck dinner. His employer, Aspen Meadows Resort, donated the turkeys.
PAUL ANDERSEN/ASPEN JOURNALISM

wanted to invite people who are new to the valley, like seasonal employees who might not have a big kitchen at home where they can make a really big meal and might not have many people to share it with," Bernhardt said. "We wanted to create a space where people could come and enjoy a meal with others and enjoy their company, and especially enjoy the holidays."

"Nicholas thought it was a great idea," said Bernhardt, "so we hit the ground running, and the volunteers have done an absolutely incredible job providing real plates and real silverware and a chef and all the donated food. I am really happy to be here and happy to celebrate with everyone."

Jeff Spiroff, banquet chef at the Aspen Meadows Resort, volunteered to oversee preparations for the feast.

"Nicholas and I brainstormed the idea of hosting those who didn't have a holiday table to go to this Christmas," Spiroff said while busily dishing out turkey from a huge platter, "so we reached out to single kids who work for the Aspen Skiing Co. and who need a holiday table.

We got the congregation together and decided to collectively host a potluck. I asked the Aspen Meadows Resort to donate six turkeys, and it all came together."

Most of the guests were new to Aspen, Snowmass and the Roaring Fork Valley, far from family and friends, and most had not yet had a homestyle dinner prepared for them here with love and community in mind.

"This is the epitome of community," said Michael Glah, a lifelong resident of Aspen and an Aspen Chapel regular. "It's great that the chapel hosted this for the SkiCo kids who are super-far away from home and don't get to have a legitimate home-cooked meal. One of the kids at our table said he had been living on frozen pizzas for the last month because that's all he could afford. And many of them spend so much time commuting. For them, this is a really cool experience. They heard about it from a friend of a friend of a friend, and this is really special for describing what community means."

When the buffet line opened, there was a miniscrum toward the food tables. Soon, diners were carrying off plates heaped with turkey, salad, vegetables and mashed potatoes with steaming turkey gravy. There were smiles of good tidings all around.

As the diners got down to business, a hush fell over the room until folk singer Dan Sheridan struck up the chords to Christmas carols sung by one and all with equal measures of spirit and hilarity. A good time was had by guests and hosts alike in what may become a chapel tradition of hospitality and generosity, both hallmarks of the holiday spirit. "This is important to me personally," said Bernhardt, who noted that he has never initiated anything like this before. "In mountain towns, it's really easy to feel loneliness and to feel a lack of community, even though there are people around you constantly. With tourists coming in, it's sometimes hard to get the feeling of a small-town community and have people to rely on, so being able to enjoy a meal with people and create an environment where people feel very comfortable is incredibly important.

Ski instructor Spencer Bernhardt inspired the Aspen Chapel Christmas potluck dinner.
PAUL ANDERSEN/ASPEN JOURNALISM

"And when the winter season really gets going," he continued, "and everything gets really exciting, people just do their work and get into the habit of getting up in the morning, working on the mountain and then going home. Having a really good meal is something people are really missing."

"This is really wonderful and really inspiring," said Jay Werner, a university student from Seattle who was in town visiting one of the chapel congregants. "It is so common to see university students struggle with loneliness. So, I'm inspired to think that maybe we could do this there. It's been a really great evening."

Aspen City Council member Ward Hauenstein was among the chapel greeters and volunteers. Looking over the roomful of holiday songsters, he smiled and said, "You hear that laughter? That's the sound of joy."

SNOWMASS POTLUCKS AND HARVEST FOR HUNGER

ON NOV. 19, 2023 the town of Snowmass Village hosted more than 100 local residents at the annual John Bemis Community Potluck at the Viewline Resort. This traditional holiday potluck began in the late 1980s as a small gathering at the Snowmass Chapel and has grown to an event that now fills a huge banquet hall.

The menu includes traditional Thanksgiving turkey, mashed potatoes and stuffing. Community members are encouraged to contribute side dishes. The Snowmass community also brings nonperishable food items for Harvest for Hunger, a Snowmass-based nonprofit that collects food from grocery stores and restaurants from Aspen to Carbondale—food that would otherwise go to waste. These collections then go to distribution partners and local agencies to provide food for those in need across the Western Slope of Colorado.

Aspen Chapel minister Nicholas Vesey gave a holiday blessing to a group of mostly seasonal workers who turned up for the chapel's Christmas potluck dinner on Dec. 17.
PAUL ANDERSEN/ASPEN JOURNALISM

Launched in 2020 "by ski bums," according to the website, who live and work in the Roaring Fork Valley, Harvest for Hunger has become a noted food-distribution source in just three years. Founder Gray Warr said he recognized a disconnect in the valley between the fortunate and the less fortunate where many families struggle with wage disparity and the high cost of living, and where food can often be in short supply.

Harvest for Hunger was recently featured on National Public Radio's show All Things Considered, thanks to an interview conducted by Kaya Williams, a reporter for NPR affiliate Aspen Public Radio. The story was picked up nationally, and for good reason. The charitable act of providing free food is a perfect complement to holidays associated with giving, which seems hard-wired into Warr's philanthropic nature and extended sense of community.

Gray Warr founded Harvest for Hunger, a Snowmass-based nonprofit, after he recognized a disconnect in the valley between the fortunate and the less fortunate. CONTRIBUTED PHOTO

"I was a ski instructor with clients who offered food leftovers when their vacations ended," Warr said. "I reached out to other instructors for the same, thinking that those leftovers could be distributed to the needy."

But leftovers often proved unacceptable, so, thanks to advice and encouragement from Katherine Sands of Aspen Family Connections, Warr shifted to larger food donors such as grocery stores.

"I started with City Market in Aspen," Warr said, "then went to the City Markets at Carbondale and El Jebel, then expanded to Whole Foods, Roxy's, Louis Swiss Bakery, Paradise Bakery, Clark's Market in Aspen and Snowmass, the Limelight Hotel in Aspen and Snowmass, then the Hotel Jerome, Aspen Meadows Resort, Little Nell, and the Food & Wine and Ideas festivals.

I didn't know what I was getting myself into, and it has grown." Warr describes Harvest for Hunger as a middleman that delivers goods to Food Bank of the Rockies in Grand Junction and to Lift-Up in Parachute. "As partners, we deliver and they distribute across the Western Slope to food pantries."

Warr said Harvest for Hunger planned to open its own pantry at Snowmass Village Town Hall starting Dec. 26, with doors and freezers open weekdays from 8:30 a.m. to 4:30 p.m. throughout the ski season.

"We will serve anyone who needs it in what I'm calling a stigma-free pantry," said Warr, "meaning that it's unsupervised, so people can come and pick up food without a stigma. Our goal is to provide food for people who need it, those who live paycheck to paycheck and may be too proud to go to a food pantry. We will also be open to the undocumented because no identity is needed."

Warr's civil service background grew out of the five years he worked in disaster relief for the Federal Emergency Management Agency. He noticed the food lines at distribution centers. "Seeing all this available food here, I decided now was the time. I'm so excited to get our pantry open the day after Christmas, and I'm especially grateful to the town of Snowmass Village and to the local grocery stores."

Deborah Madsen of Snowmass Village is launching the "Kind Neighbor Project" to serve the town's youthful and often-at-risk workforce.
CONTRIBUTED PHOTO

"KIND NEIGHBOR PROJECT" PROVIDES COMMUNITY FOR SKICO WORKFORCE

DEBORAH MADSEN, a longtime resident of Snowmass Village, recently knocked on every door at the Club Commons, a SkiCo employee housing complex, and handed out cookies. In a personal, caring manner and with motherly concern, she checked in with these young residents, many of whom are newcomers to the Roaring Fork Valley.

"We get all these incredible new people who come to our town, at least 1,200," said Madsen, wife of Snowmass Village Mayor Billy Madsen, "and when they get here they don't always have bedding, cooking utensils and warm clothes, and they don't know anyone. They don't have family, so I want to create a neighbor-to-neighbor project where members of our community will reach out to these kids to meet them, maybe give them a place at their table, or give them a ride or even just provide laundry detergent—we're talking the basics."

Madsen's concern has grown over the years after witnessing police interventions and ambulance visits for this youthful and often-at-risk workforce. "If we get them involved in our community early on, we can avoid some of the problems that can happen with illicit drugs, depression and police calls," she said.

"I have had calls from parents who say, 'My child is really sick, I don't know a doctor there and I don't know what to do.' So, I went to the Commons and found this kid and took him to the clinic at Snowmass. Then I went home and made a pot of soup and hot tea and cookies." Madsen learned that the young man had roommates who were also in need. "He said the doors to their rooms were closed and they were always on their phone. I realized that these kids are lonely, and I don't feel that anyone in our community should be lonely. By creating a sense of community, I'm hoping we can alleviate those things. And there are a lot of people living here who need a sense of community as well."

To that end, Madsen is orchestrating a program of weekly potluck dinners at the Snowmass Chapel where the chapel purchases food for a main course and community members contribute side dishes. Some provisions will come from Harvest for Hunger's larder. Madsen said, "We're calling it the Kind Neighbor Project," a community- building effort based on nourishment and well-being. "It's all run by volunteers, where the kids we serve bring a dish and community members bring a dish, and it gives us a chance to sit around and talk. By doing these meals, hopefully we will create community for them."

The potlucks are being planned at the Snowmass Chapel every Thursday during the ski season starting Jan. 11 from 5 to 7 p.m., an ambitious logistical challenge. Yet, Madsen's personal mission goes further still. Donating money to the cause is appreciated, but that's not enough, said Madsen. "I don't want people to just throw money at it; I want them to volunteer. I want them to give back," she said. "When I handed out over 300 cookies, I knocked on every single door at the Commons. And the kids said, 'Oh, wow, thank you! This is a nice place!'

"A lot of these kids will only be here for one season, so let's make it a good one for them, one that's not lonely, that's not depressing, that's not drunken or stoned the whole time. This close-knit community can help alleviate some of the loneliness."

CHAPTER 3

Aspen's First Embattled Communities

*Eviction of the Utes
and the Crash of Silver*

AUTHOR'S NOTE: The following four installments
provide a close focus on Aspen's evolving community
because the city's historic socio-economic development
has influenced the entire region and continues to play
a signficant role in many of today's community challenges.
Understanding the arc of Aspen's history
is necessary to understanding the region.

As miners followed silver veins into the earth, large caverns, or stopes, were opened and stabilized by post-and-beam frameworks processed at Aspen sawmills from wood harvested from clearcut local forests.
ASPEN HISTORICAL SOCIETY

TODAY'S HAND-WRINGING over the lost soul or vanquished spirit of Aspen is nothing new. Such laments have echoed throughout every epoch in Aspen's storied past. This doesn't diminish the shared sense of loss felt by Aspenites when familiarity with what they love is eroded or erased. Rather, it reveals a continuum of attachment to a place and a time that has never been and never can be static.

Aspen's community has proved resilient despite dramatic changes that have long inflamed a cathartic sense of loss. Aspenites are contentious about change because change alters the experience that first gave them a rich sense of place. A first love of Aspen leaves a deep emotional imprint.

The shifting fortunes of Aspen over the past 145 years of its written history have made community identity a constant challenge. Historical context is critical to an understanding of community, and that must begin with the Utes—the People of the Shining Mountains—who were the first population to experience an embattled community in the Roaring Fork Valley.

THE NATIVE COMMUNITY INHABITED THIS LAND FOR THOUSANDS OF YEARS

THE FIRST PEOPLE to see this country came upon it 10,000 to 12,000 years ago, at the end of the Wisconsin Ice Age, after early man had crossed the Bering Strait on a land or ice bridge between the continents of Asia and North America. These paleo hunters pursued a moving banquet of mammoth and buffalo that followed the warming sun south along the foothills of the Rocky Mountains.

Not far from the Roaring Fork Valley, "Timberline Man" was discovered in 1989 by spelunkers in a cave in the White River National Forest. Dated to 8,000 years ago, this paleo-Indian was studied in

Washington, D.C., then returned to Colorado, where the Utes, claiming him as an early ancestor, interred the ancient remains with a sacred ceremony. The cave has been sealed and the location has been kept a secret.

Yarmony, a prehistoric pit house site, was discovered during a highway excavation near State Bridge, along the Colorado River, in 1987. These remains, dated to 7,000 years ago, show that early man not only migrated through the region, but left permanent residences.

Ute tipis were the valley's original affordable housing and horses were the first conveyances for these master horsemen. ASPEN HISTORICAL SOCIETY MASTERSON ESTATE COLLECTION

The native Utes have been linked with the Paiutes of Utah. Both share common ancestry with the Fremont people of the Great Basin and the northern Colorado Plateau. The Utes spent summers in the Roaring Fork Valley hunting and gathering as a Stone Age, tribal culture. Acquiring the horse in the early 1600s from the Spaniards afforded the Utes mobility for hunting and warring, and they secured for their domain most of the Colorado Rockies, extending east onto the high plains, where they hunted buffalo. Their empire stretched to present-day Texas, Wyoming, Utah, Nebraska and Kansas.

The Utes celebrated a spiritual connection with the natural world in a tribal life that relied upon mutual support at every level. Their homes were tipis covered with skins, or wickiups made from a frame of sticks and branches covered with brush or skins. Housing for the nomadic Utes was recycled, organic, biodegradable, affordable and portable.

The Utes were people of the seasons who roamed the valleys and the high mountains, danced for the bear as it came out of hibernation, heralded the deep voice of thunder and raised their faces to the lightning flash. A dependence on nature cultivated a deep sense of respect and belonging to the world around them. Such was the extended community in which they embraced pristine nature within a theology that made sacred the elemental forces under the thrall of which they worshipped a pantheon of nature spirits. Their homeland was their church, their prayer circles their chapels, the sky their cathedral domes, the earth their mother, and the heavens their father. They were children of air, water, earth and fire. Fiercely independent, the Utes faced an inexorable foe with the advancing tsunami of white European settlers who eventually sought to banish them from their traditional lands across most of western Colorado.

When the Ferdinand Vandeveer Hayden survey team explored the Roaring Fork Valley in the summers of 1873-74, it was as if aliens had arrived from another planet. Hayden had been nicknamed "crazy man who picks up rocks" by other Native Americans who had witnessed the scientist's rock collecting as insane antics. When Hayden's geologic surveys were made available in the late 1870s, they became treasure maps for a throng of wealth-seekers who recklessly violated treaties and willfully trespassed on Ute lands under the entitlement of Manifest Destiny.

This set up the inevitable clash between industrial resource exploitation and the comparatively harmonic ecological balance extant within the realm of the Utes. Confined by ever-constricting relocations and jaded by broken treaties, the Utes were pushed to the brink of tolerance. They finally snapped under the authority of Indian agent Nathan Meeker. His efforts to convert these hunter-gatherers into farmers culminated with the plowing under of the Utes' horse racetrack, which was an affront to this equestrian people. Even more so was Meeker's call for U.S. cavalry backup in bad faith to Ute leaders. When those troops crossed into Ute territory, Ute fighters—believing the incursion to be an act of war that meant the slaughter of their people was at hand—killed Meeker and 10 of his male agency staffers in 1879.

This provided grounds for a "final solution" edict issued by Colorado Governor Frederick Pitkin:

"My idea is that, unless removed by the government, the Ute Indians must necessarily be exterminated. The state would be willing to settle the Indian trouble at its own expense. The advantages that would be accrued from the throwing open of 12 million acres of land to miners and settlers would more than compensate all expenses incurred."

In 1881, the disenfranchised Utes were force-marched from their traditional lands and suffered the first crisis of community in our region. Here was the Cain and Abel story told against the backdrop of Western settlement where the hunter-gatherer was slain by the farmer, the townsite planner, the railroad builder and the mining speculator. Cain murdered Abel in the "Shining Mountains" of Colorado, and the Roaring Fork Valley was opened for business.

Underground mining work was laborious and dangerous. Here a drill team bores holes for dynamite charges. ASPEN HISTORICAL SOCIETY

A NEW COMMUNITY SEEKS RICHES

IN 1879, two years before the Utes were removed to reservations, prospectors had pushed into the upper Roaring Fork Valley over its high passes. Unlike most mountain valleys, the Roaring Fork Valley was settled first from its headwaters because of obstacles in the lower valley: treaty land held by the Utes and the formidable abyss of Glenwood Canyon.

When two prospecting parties in 1879 coincidentally made camp together at Ute Spring at the base of Aspen Mountain, near today's Gant Condominiums, they gathered around a campfire and made a vow of mutual protection of themselves and their unproved mining claims. Eager to secure their lives and their interests, this tacit agreement was the settlers' first political exercise in Aspen, creating the civic foundation for a community founded on silver.

Crossing the high routes into the Roaring Fork Valley required grit and determination, the requisite character traits of Aspen's silver seekers. This unifying identity instilled a hard-bitten resolve necessary during the mining era when community was solidified by the

An Aspen mine hoist provided a framework from which ore buckets were lifted from the depths of a shaft and were powered by hydroelectric energy. ASPEN HISTORICAL SOCIETY SHAW COLLECTION

brutal labor of tunneling into mountains following veins of ore and by the rigors of surviving on the edge of wilderness at 8,000 feet. Slowly, the Aspen community expanded with the advent of businesses that supported mining and profited from it. This formed a social division of miners and merchants where the former exploited the earth and the latter exploited the former.

A townsite dispute between two town founders, B. Clark Wheeler and Henry Gillespie, caused a split that alienated half the nascent city from the other, as claimants sought political hegemony and profitable land sales. Soon resolved amicably in Wheeler's favor so the community could advance, a second and more intractable legal problem arose known as the Apex controversy. This issue instigated complex litigation that challenged mining claims and held up mine development for four years. Aspenites were again divided. "High stakes raised the level of greed, already well developed in the mining camps," wrote historian Malcolm Rohrbough in *Aspen: The History of a Silver Mining Town*, and drove a wedge into the struggling camp.

The Apex controversy was settled with a compromise just as two competing railroads pushed their tracks into Aspen in 1887-88. A new industrial era dawned, and with it an increasingly complex community divided by subsets based on ethnicity, religion, fraternal organizations and labor unions that represented the professional miner: "men with similar skills and needs and, above all, with a common identity," wrote Rohrbough.

Industrial mining was a far cry from the romantic image of the pick-and-shovel prospector with his burro and a gold pan strapped across his pack saddle. The romance ended once the ore was found. Then came the mechanics of blasting the rock, excavating the shafts, mapping the veins, and processing and shipping the ore. Aspen quickly became part of mainstream industrial America once its ore-rich mountains were a known quantity.

The whistles blew, the shifts changed, and the men marched to and from work. They carried lunch pails and wore leather helmets affixed with headlamps. They were the minions of industry and they faced numerous dangers in the mines where injury and illness awaited them in the dark, wet tunnels and tomblike stopes they drove, like trolls, deeper and deeper into the earth.

They lived humbly and worked for scant daily wages of $1 to $3. They worked long hours to bring home enough to feed and clothe a family, to make payments on their homes and to enjoy a beer or two at their favorite saloon. They fed coal into their stoves, where they warmed their hands on cold winter days before starting a shift.

Mines were dark, dank and dangerous. The deeper the mine went, the hotter it became, and men worked stripped to the waist. Candles flickered on the walls and the air was filled with dust and stench. The miners endured bruised and battered hands, cold, wet feet and lungs coated with particulates that plagued them with "miner's consumption." The monotonous nature of the work and fatigue from hard physical labor created lethargy that resulted in carelessness and deadly mistakes.

Miners unable to see through the murk could fall more than 100 feet down a shaft or air vent. Body retrievals were grim and time-consuming. Dynamite and blasting caps were in constant use, and misfirings caused deaths and injuries, including lost hands, mangled arms and blindness. There were cave-ins and toxic gas seeps. In 1891-92, miners died at the rate of roughly one a month. Injuries were far more frequent. The wealth of the mine owners was born by the misery of the laborers.

Who were the Aspenites making up the industrial mining community? Aspen's 1885 census (three years before the railroads) reported the population was 72.4% male and 99% white, with a handful of blacks, mulattos and Indians but no Asians. Germans and Irish were most heavily represented, with mixes of English, Scots and Welsh. Counted among Aspen residents were 810 miners and 115 prospectors; 12 mine engineers; 8 mine superintendents; 39 smelter workers; 6 charcoal burners; 26 sawmill workers; 3 contractors; 9 painters; 9 brick masons; 20 grocers; 20 butchers; 55 teamsters; 60 freighters; 35 blacksmiths; 8 doctors; 31 lawyers; 4 school teachers; 12 real estate brokers; 22 hotel keepers; 16 barbers; 22 cooks; 48 laundresses; 41 saloonkeepers; 31 bartenders; 4 prostitutes; 8 gamblers; and 5 actresses.

In Aspen's early years, before pressurized fire hydrants, hose cart companies joined men in harnesses to sprint through the streets to a fire where the team was then tasked to pumping water from strategically located cisterns. ASPEN HISTORICAL SOCIETY SHAW COLLECTION

In Aspen's earliest days, civic bonds were formed through social activities instituted as an antidote to the deep isolation of this remote mountain redoubt. Baseball, a new national identity, became popular among "miners, mechanics, teamsters, carpenters and draymen," wrote Rohrbough. "Some played and others watched, but all groups talked, joked, ate and drank" with the deepening of community ties.

Hose-cart brigades put men together in harness for the protection of their stick-built city. Dances, socials, theater, churches, political parties, charities and a temperance union joined the people in shared pursuits toward a better life. For the many single men who labored in the tunnels, gambling, saloons and prostitutes provided recreation and challenged the moral authority of town builders. Beer consumption in 1885 grew from 30 barrels a day in winter to 45 barrels a day in summer, eliciting wonder at the freighters who drove teams and wagons over Independence Pass to provide provisions before the railroads arrived.

Drink was but one of the collateral human costs on this industrial frontier. Other costs could be seen in the desperate eyes of prostitutes loitering in the red-light district near the Colorado Midland station along the base of Aspen Mountain. A large contingent of single working men was mired in drunkenness and destitution in the saloons, their wages gulped down in shot glasses and frothing beer, their nights spent in bordellos and boarding houses. They were written up in police records for brawls, assaults, thefts and murders.

Pack trains of donkeys and mules were the motive force for transporting goods into Aspen over the high passes and supplying prospectors and miners at remote mine sites. This train is seen setting off from downtown Aspen in the mid-1880s. ASPEN HISTORICAL SOCIETY SHAW COLLECTION

By the time the mines were running at full bore in the early 1890s, the native elk herds had been exterminated by overhunting, and streams and lakes were depleted of trout. All of nature's bounty was destined to feed man's insatiable appetites, and there was no effort toward sustainability. When the wild meat ran out, pioneer ranchers provided beef by grazing cattle on the mountains and raising hay in the valleys. Farmers grew potatoes. The rivers were drawn low for irrigation and flowed through ingenious systems of ditches. Some of the waters were so polluted with industrial waste that they weren't suitable for irrigation. Silver production was the religion, the earth was the altar and profits were the salvation—all sought with unbridled human enterprise and expense.

Historic Aspen is often seen through the idealized chimera of gigantic silver nuggets in the backs of wagons, of festive street parades, of steam locomotives chugging along scenic grades, and of pageantry and boomtown opulence. Look deeper. There, hidden in the background of old daguerreotype photographs is a gritty side that expresses a simple equation: With every ounce of silver taken from the bowels of the Elk Mountains came a quantity of blood, travail and ecological devastation. The Utes were the first victims of industrial mining; the community of miners was the second.

Meanwhile, a small set of wealthy elites—the mine and railroad owners and investors—represented capital and Eastern influence. They established refined cultural amenities, including a fine hotel and an opera house that stood out against the contrast of the rugged frontier. "The fertile imaginations of Aspen's socially minded citizens generated innumerable reasons for social gatherings," wrote Rohrbough, who described a burgeoning sense of pride in the civilizing influences of a community hewn out of the wilderness. "Social and cultural life at all levels was built on a foundation of prosperity, progress, development and growth."

The pace was slow enough, wrote Rohrbough, to keep Aspen attractive. "Part of the appeal of the city lay in its initial slow growth. The gradual evolution of Aspen stood in vivid contrast to the helter-skelter and uncontrolled development of Leadville. Aspen had both economic prosperity and an appealing place to live."

In 1893, Aspen was touted as the greatest mining center in the world, wrote Rohrbough, with 227 developed mines and 2,500 professional miners working for $3 a day. The population was 12,000, in addition to roughly 5,000 transients. There were two major banks, two broad-gauge railroads that brought 10 passenger trains and four freight trains daily and the third-largest opera house in the state. The Hotel Jerome was reputed to be the finest luxury hotel on the Western Slope. Aspen was a sophisticated city that had waterworks, electric light, hydroelectric power, a hospital, streetcars, public schools and nine newspapers that operated at some point between 1886 and 1893.

A visual reflection of Aspen's community from the mining era is seen in the torchlight parades that today flow in a stream of light down Aspen Mountain for special events with torch-bearing skiers. That spectacle revisits the miners lighting their way back down into town during shift changes at night with mining helmets and lanterns—men who made the Aspen community function yet who are mostly lost from the historic record.

"The emergence of socioeconomic distinctions in Aspen, the several identifiable ethnic groups, the competing religious denominations and the growing differences in wealth tended to divide and fragment the community," wrote Rohrbough. Unity, he wrote, came through boosterism, the promotion of Aspen's growth and prosperity "in which all individuals and all groups presumably had a common interest. Another unifying feature was the residual frontier instinct to come together in the face of disaster—fires, blizzards, avalanches and mining accidents— with an outpouring of common assistance and genuine concern that transcended group identification."

This altruistic virtue of community largesse prompted the formation in 1886 of the Pioneer Association, which honored Aspen's original "locals"—those who came before the fall of 1881. The association would "perpetuate the bonds of union made memorable by the struggles, trials and hopes of the early days of Aspen . . . to cultivate a spirit of sociability among those who tramped over the Indian trails to plant the foundations of a new empire in the then-wilderness of the Roaring Fork Valley."

The largest silver nugget ever mined in the United States, 1800 pounds and 90% silver, came from the Smuggler Mine in 1894.
ASPEN HISTORICAL SOCIETY

The silver crash of 1893, perpetrated when the U.S. government elected to no longer back its currency with silver, shattered the Aspen mining community by drastically undermining the economic foundation upon which Aspen was built. There were other local and regional mining activities—iron ore in Cooper Basin south of Ashcroft; peachblow sandstone and limestone up the Fryingpan Valley; coal in Coal Basin west of Redstone and at New Castle—but too distant from Aspen to defray the loss of silver, the city's lifeblood. Some silver mining continued, but prices fluctuated dramatically. Aspen never regained its mining boom.

The following dirge from a departing miner poeticizes the lament for a lost community that succumbed to external influences that were beyond local control. Such was the toll from socioeconomic dependence on a volatile and speculative extractive industry. The silver crash was the second crisis for Aspen's embattled community.

Now I sit on the porch and watch the lightning-bugs fly.

But I can't see too good, I got tears in my eyes.

I'm leaving tomorrow, but I don't wanna go.

I love you, my town, you'll always live in my soul.

But I can see the sun's settin' fast,

And just like they say, nothing good ever lasts.

Well, go on, and kiss it goodbye,

But hold to your memories,

'Cause my heart's 'bout to die.

Go on now and say goodbye to our town, to our town.

I can see the sun has gone down on our town, on our town,

Goodnight.

—WILLIAM ZAUGG
Zaugg Dump is an Aspen Mountain
double-black diamond ski run

Farming and ranching became mainstays of the economy of the Roaring Fork Valley during the Quiet Years.
ASPEN HISTORICAL SOCIETY

CHAPTER 4

The "Quiet Years" of Aspen

"A simpler, kinder, egalitarian Aspen"

IF YOU WERE IN ASPEN in March 2020, when the emerging COVID-19 pandemic shut down the ski mountains and stymied the regional economy, you will have a sense for the Quiet Years when shocked citizens witnessed industrial mining go from boom to bust overnight, leaving farming and ranching as the mainstays for a struggling rural economy. Most of the miners left Aspen for other prospects, leaving a skeletal community that stuck resolutely to their beloved Aspen.

"My favorite years in Aspen were in the '30s and '40s," recalled Ellamae Huffine Phillips in *Aspen: The Quiet Years,* by Kathleen Krieger Daily and Gaylord Guenin, "because everyone was in the same class—we were all poor." Rather than the promise of riches, the Aspen community was reduced to one common denominator—poverty—perhaps the most cohesive influence the Aspen community has ever had.

"The lights of Aspen began to dim and softly flicker for almost 50 years," according to *The Quiet Years*. "Still, the lights never went out. These were the years between prospecting and prosperity. We call them the Quiet Years. A town without a tomorrow, from about 1893 to 1947, Aspen's only future lay in its past. All of its dreams were trapped in its memories of yesterday.

Aspen's boomtown population peaked in 1893 at about 12,000 when 227 working mines made Aspen one of the richest silver mining districts in the world. That was the year the U.S. Congress repealed the Sherman Silver Purchase Act, which ended the free coinage of silver, removed the silver standard, crippled the populist movement and made gold the basis of the U.S. dollar. That was the year Aspen suffered a crushing blow from which the industrialized economy of the famed "Crystal City" would never recover.

"The Quiet Years," a paean to desolation, despair and yet to a stern, unyielding community character stated, "Aspen was knocked to its knees. Here was a community that knew only one thing—silver." Without silver, the community was left to languish in obscurity. The geographic isolation that had beset early Aspen was now compounded by a lack of promise and purpose. All that was left was community.

A dramatic exodus left Aspen's population at 750 or fewer. "I can tell you that in the 1930s, there weren't more than 350 in this town,"

The Veteran Tunnel, as seen in winter, 1950, reveals the overlap of mining and recreation as two skiers make their way down Aspen Mountain in front of the mine structures. The Veteran Tunnel was part of the Aspen Mine complex. ASPEN HISTORICAL SOCIETY

said an anonymous source in *The Quiet Years*. "I knew everybody in town. Hell, I knew the name of every damn dog in town, too." Those who stayed knew that Aspen was down, but it was not out. An intangible and intractable community bond buoyed the hangers-on.

Amid the collective sorrow, sparks of light came with hope, strength and resilience. Almost 20 years after the crash, a speculative mining venture called the Hope Tunnel promised to resuscitate the city with the ever-bright promise of a motherlode. A shaft was begun in 1911 atop Richmond Ridge that was to tap the silver resources beneath Little Annie Basin. Mining commenced, and two train carloads of ore were optimistically shipped. Then calamity struck in 1929 when a fire destroyed the newly constructed mill and most of the surface structures. Silence again fell over the beleaguered city.

"The community of Aspen became dominated by abandoned homes, boarded up businesses and collapsing mine shafts," according to *The Quiet Years*. "Nature slowly reclaimed the mountains." Whole blocks were vacant. Some abandoned structures were stripped to bare framing as opportunists made off with materials for their own homes or for resale. Many miners' shacks were stripped down to nothing and were gone.

What remained was a spirited people who buried their cultural differences and came together in a pastiche of ethnic identities and colorful characters. A small listing of residents' surnames and nicknames offers a nostalgic sense of rustic charm from this little-known era: Tekoucich, Mishmash, Trentaz, Zordel, Marolt, Vagneur, Zupancis, Jakey Yeckel, Hannibal Brown, Puppy Smith, Panhandle Pete, Rattlesnake Bill Anderson, One-Eyed Joe, No Problem Joe, Groundhog Joe, Horse Thief Kelly, Tom the Weasel, The Whispering Swedes, and Chicken Bill.

The original Anderson Ranch at Snowmass in 1940. It is summer time, and several buildings are visible across a field with a horse in it. Mt. Daly can be seen in the background. ASPEN HISTORICAL SOCIETY GROVER COLLECTION

"Even with ramshackle buildings and vacant lots," a subject interviewed for "The Quiet Years" reflected, "there was something always here—a resurgence. Where there was a cabin, there might be an aspen tree starting up through the floorboards... Growth came back."

A newspaper editorial in December 1929, at the onset of the Great Depression, set an optimistic tone for community spirit: "Christmas Day in Aspen was an ideal winter day ... and the Christmas spirit reigned supreme ... Everyone glad and happy and full of the spirit of doing good unto others." This echo of the Lord's Prayer evinced a resolute ethic that infused a tottering Aspen with respect and esteem. None of it had to do with wealth or pretense or status. "Not a selfish thought or act bobbed up in this beautiful mining camp ... Not a family that went without their Christmas dinner ... not a child that Santa didn't remember... not an empty stocking. And that's Aspen!"

The Hotel Jerome became a community focal point as a residence hotel for those whose homes lacked central heating and indoor plumbing—and there were many such homes. There were no tourists then to compete for limited space, and everyone knew one another from close proximity and shared meals in the dining room. Perhaps the only new arrivals to seek a home in Aspen was an elk herd imported by rail in the 1920s from Idaho to replace the native herds that had been exterminated during the mining boom.

Despite the city's dismal prospects, celebrations were held, in-

David Robinson Crocker (DRC) Brown (1856-1930) holds his son, also named DRC Brown, Jr. (1912-2007). The son would become the president of the Aspen Ski Company from 1958 to 1979, after Aspen transitioned from mining to recreation. The father was one of Aspen's most prominent and influential Aspen pioneers, arriving by wagon over Taylor Pass in June 1880. ASPEN HISTORICAL SOCIETY SHAW COLLECTION

cluding dances and social events at outlying school houses, in empty barns or at private homes where neighbors threw out the welcome mat. The Elks and Eagles clubs organized picnics and outings. Ice skating, roller skating, sleigh rides and skiing brought people together. A flower show symbolized the city's resurgent essence. Merchants extended credit to provide the necessities. Bootleggers defied Prohibition to keep spirits up. Families collected berries and mushrooms. Hunters and fishermen provided what they could.

When town father and Aspen pioneer David R.C. Brown died in 1930, a miles long funeral procession ushered his remains over Independence Pass, commemorating his many achievements and saluting the halcyon mining years when well-meaning, ambitious, hardworking and talented men such as Brown could become millionaires.

"The emphasis on community and family was dominant," according to *The Quiet Years*.

Humility, rather than hubris, had cultivated perhaps the most unifying social cohesion Aspen has ever displayed.

As the Great Depression took its toll on Aspen, outside eyes began to recognize something in the dissolute city that could become fertile ground for a new era. Interest in skiing took root, first in Ashcroft in the 1930s, then with the cutting of Roche Run on Aspen Mountain by Works Progress Administration (WPA) crews in 1937 under the auspices of the Roaring Fork Winter Sports Club, later named the Aspen Valley Ski Club (AVSC). Roche Run was designed by Swiss ski maestro Andre Roche. It was served by the "boat tow," a toboggan pulled up the mountain by an old mining winch. A ride cost a dime.

Skiing in a commercial sense was barely off the ground in Aspen when, in 1941, the National Alpine Championships were held on Aspen Mountain. Enthused skiers began singing Aspen's praises as the next big attraction for lovers of snow, speed and a quaint, refreshing atmosphere.

On Dec. 7 of that year, the Japanese bombed Pearl Harbor. Grandiose ski dreams for Ashcroft and Mount Hayden were irrevocably derailed while, across the Continental Divide in Leadville, a new breed of skiers donned white anoraks to become the country's first military ski troops—the 10th Mountain Division. Many of these mountain soldiers would move to Aspen after the war to become founders of the Colorado ski industry, infusing the Aspen community with notoriety and a rambunctious sense of frivolity.

Two men, two women, and a dog in front of the Hunter Creek Dam, 1917. ASPEN HISTORICAL SOCIETY

When the war ended in 1945, America shifted into high gear with an exuberance that was perfectly suited to Aspen's potential, something that Chicago industrialist Walter Paepcke would astutely recognize. He wasn't alone. Radio personality Lowell Thomas was among the early skiers who became an ardent Aspen booster. In 1939, Walter's wife, Elizabeth Paepcke, had also recognized a gem in the rough in Aspen's well-preserved cityscape, a relic of past glory that became attractive to cognoscenti who saw potential in its tarnished charm.

On her ski run down Aspen Mountain, Elizabeth Paepcke gazed upon dormant Aspen and worded a now-famous telephone message to her husband, Chicago industrialist Walter Paepcke: "Walter, you simply must see it. It's the most beautifully untouched place in the world." With that invitation, Elizabeth Paepcke initiated dramatic changes in the nascent ski town and emergent cultural center when she returned to Aspen six years later with her visionary and opportunistic husband.

In a speech to an Aspen audience decades later, Elizabeth recalled that visit with Walter and her parents in the summer of 1945, a trip they made at her urging. This was Walter's first view of what Elizabeth had so memorably beheld in 1939:

> In those days, Aspen had a different appearance. Along the two sides of every street ran irrigation ditches constantly flowing with water. The cottonwoods, which drew their nourishment from this source, grew strong and tall. One walked in pleasant, leafy shade. Because no street was paved or winter-plowed, the ruts were deep and, where not overgrown with grass, the walking could be tricky and also extremely dusty.
>
> Between the tangle of cottonwoods, ancient lilacs and orchard grass, we could see ruins of collapsing wooden houses, quite beautiful with gables and fretwork carved like lace. Here a door was missing, there a roof gaped. Shutters hung on broken hinges and porches sagged. We looked through broken glass into parlors still carpeted, where flowered paper hung in sad festoons and sofas oozed their horsehair stuffing onto the floor to mingle with long-discarded newsprint. It was a town unspoiled, untouched since 1893, when the collapse of silver placed it in a state of uneasy, somnambulistic shock.
>
> During our leisurely saunter along Main Street on that sunny day, we saw nothing move, nothing that seemed alive, until near the Jerome Hotel where we stumbled upon a woman's body, half-reclining in the gutter, not dead, only sodden. Where the Ute City Banque now flourishes, to our joy, at last, we saw two human beings very alive and both very drunk. They sat by an irrigation ditch very happily soaking their bare feet while singing irreverent songs.
>
> As my mother approached, both men rose and clutched at her frantically. She was the one stable object on their otherwise reeling horizon. They tried to explain to my fascinated parents through toothless gums that their condition was not normal, but was arrived at by celebrating a wake—their mother's. That in the interest of safety, they had

stowed their false teeth in mugs before the festivities began and were now sitting in the ditch waiting for the return of sobriety.

My father was not amused, my mother was full of sympathy, but I noticed that Walter Paepcke became ominously silent on the way home. In this fashion, even out of irrigation ditches, great ideas sometime emerge.

In a 2019 speech at the Aspen Institute, James Sloane Allen, author of *The Romance of Commerce and Culture,* recounted: "Elizabeth had ventured here on skis and had described it as a Sleeping Beauty waiting to awaken. Walter had never been here when he hatched the idea of buying some vacant Aspen properties as investments or vacation homes for his family and friends and other 'high type of persons,' as he liked to label them."

Despite decades of neglect that had left a layer of grime on old Aspen and a pall of quiet over the potholed and dusty dirt streets, Aspen had charm. Its eerie museum quality, frozen in time, appealed to the husband and wife visionaries. Aspen was as enchanting as anything Elizabeth Paepcke had ever seen, and she was totally taken by it. What she discovered in Aspen was the chemistry that so often describes the first meeting of lovers—a physical attraction of bodies, an emotional gravity that binds and holds.

As the Quiet Years drew to a close in the late 1940s, this Shangri-la would be discovered in a crescendo of ardent lovers whose energy, enterprise and imagination gradually formed the foundation of a new community girded by commercialism that has grown steadily for 80 years and shows no signs of letting up.

CHAPTER 5

Skiing and Culture Define Aspen's Future

The birth and growth of Aspen's resort economy

Aspen quickly became synonymous with superb, world class skiing, shown here In the 1940s when ski equipment was primitive compared to today,
ASPEN HISTORICAL SOCIETY KAESER COLLECTION

A SPEN IN THE LATE 1940S was fertile ground for a renaissance based on a curious mixture of skiing and high-minded culture. The reborn city on the hill rose up from the ruins of a prior culture, and those ruins provided the fecund compost for a revived culture to take root and grow. Aspen was to completely shift from an industrial economy and, in the prophetic words of Walter Paepcke, nurture the pursuit of the "good life through the sharing of ideas that are more important to the preservation of our society and our liberties than the ceaseless striving for material gain."

Silver mining was gone. The Quiet Years were at an end. Aspen found itself at a new crossroads. The Aspen community eyed, to borrow words from Robert Frost, a road not taken—one that "was grassy and wanted wear," a road that would lead into the distant glimmer of an unknown and unplanned future. The unlikely guide was a brainiac from Chicago who plotted a very unusual course.

Peggy Clifford, in her 1970 book, "Aspen: Dreams and Dilemmas," described Walter Paepcke this way: "A medium-sized, sharp-featured man with calm, blue eyes, who always looked a little awkward when he smiled. Paepcke moved quietly about Aspen—usually dressed in tweed coat, sports shirt and flannel trousers—tending to his properties, his projects, his visions. There was something outsized about both the man and his dream, but the character of the dream was always easier to analyze than the character of the man. He made decisions quickly, he spoke with assurance, and he always kept a little distance between himself and most of the townspeople."

In a speech to Aspen Institute trustees in 2009, James Sloane Allen said, "Aspen was a quiet, long-faded but well-preserved silver-mining boom town when Walter Paepcke set his sights on it at the end of World War II. He sensed an economic and social opportunity for the postwar years, but he didn't want to tip his hand lest landowners catch on and prices start to rise, so he kept his intentions secret and instructed his secretary in Chicago to write to the local Aspen newspaper to inquire, in her name, where to turn 'for some friends who are somewhat interested in possibly buying an old, very cheap, but well-located vacant house, if there is such a thing in Aspen.'"

Paepcke's Aspen investments began in 1945 during his first day in Aspen, said Allen. "He had fixed his eye on dozens of houses and hundreds of lots, and he had agreed to buy the entire downtown Collins Block for $7,500. Paepcke had instructed a discreet local contact that he was 'perfectly willing to spend up to $5,000 or $6,000 at the rate of $25 a lot, but that $250 for four or five lots is pretty high.' Walter didn't even tell his wife what he was doing."

Walter Paepcke (left) oversees an historic Aspen event when the longest chairlift in the world—Lift No. 1—was opened for business in the winter of 1947. Colorado governor-elect William Lee Knous (at the microphone) gave a short speech honoring the achievement. Aspen Mayor A. E. Robison, middle, symbolically christened the lift by breaking a bottle of champagne over one of the iconic single chairs. So ended Aspen's "Quiet Years."
ASPEN HISTORICAL SOCIETY

Paepcke then went on to purchase or lease and restore much of the town, and with partners, he founded the Aspen Skiing Corporation, which marked its grand opening in January 1947 with the christening of the longest chairlift in the world. "Then, just a few weeks after this opening," Allen said, "Paepcke had a conversation with Robert Maynard Hutchins, chancellor of the University of Chicago and a close friend, that would send Aspen off in another direction." Skiing and culture were soon to redefine community in Aspen as the city welcomed two new identities.

A game-changing event came to Aspen when Paepcke and an inspired team from the University of Chicago celebrated the Goethe Bicentennial Convocation in 1949, an ambitious and defining moment in recognizing a key strategy for Aspen's long-term future: Skiing would

Dr. Albert Schweitzer was lured from Africa to Aspen in 1949 to deliver the keynote address for the Goethe Bicentennial, an auspicious event that took Aspen to its cultural zenith.
AHS HOFMANN COLLECTION

be the stabilizing influence for Aspen's economy. Culture would possess it with lofty airs.

The Goethe event conjured a utopian revelation when, for 20 days, Aspen was transformed into a philosophically inspired utopia that preached the highest expression of ethics and morality in the city's history, to date. Evelyn Ames, a participant from Long Island, New York, characterized Aspen's seminal event: "At such altitudes everything was a little sharper, in clearer focus, a little nearer the sky. Here there was no superficially cosmopolitan gathering, no arbitrary elite, but the most surprising and heady brew of Europe and the New World, of Weimar and the corner drugstore, of Goethe and cowboy boots."

Aspen had struggled in the lull between its silver mining past and its resort future, and the Goethe festival attracted the first crowd of cultural tourists to Aspen. The event was deemed an overwhelming success on which some Aspenites thought the city could capitalize in the long term. With the well-heeled Paepcke at the helm, it was time for Aspen to get down to the business of commercializing culture. In 1950, the *Aspen Times* reported a convening of Aspen decision-makers at the Four Seasons Club, which is now Aspen Country Day School and Aspen Music School campus on Castle Creek. The topic: "To Have or Not to Have?" a question offered up for discussion by Paepcke.

Paepcke had wanted a reading from city leaders as to whether Aspen would willingly host a second festival—Goethe Festival II—in the wake of the famous and inimitable first event. The resounding response of "yes" was a clear directive for Aspen to adopt the world of ideas as a launch pad for a solid tourist trade. With that unofficial vote of confidence, Aspen married economic development through cultural offerings and the glamour of skiing as a novel synthesis toward which few other resort communities had ever aspired.

"Some of the objections for Aspen having a celebration each year," reported the *Aspen Times*, "are the lack of housing, the shortage of dining space for more than ordinary crowds, disrupting the free and easy life of some few Aspenites, and generally cluttering up the streets and shops with extra people, some of them with money to spend. On the 'yes' side for Aspen is the fact that the tourist season may be lengthened ... After considerable discussion, the group voted unanimously to support in every way possible a similar celebration next year."

Instead of undergoing the Herculean labors of putting on another convocation, Paepcke and friends founded the Aspen Institute for Humanistic Studies in 1950. An institute brochure proclaimed the constitution of a new Aspen identity where "Good conversation, one of the highest achievements of reason, requires a high degree of social and intellectual community."

Here was "a unique opportunity to look with fresh eyes at the routine of one's life ... to gain a certain critical distance from which to get into better focus the dynamics of the society of which you are a part ... for American business leaders to lift their sights above the possessions which possess them, to confront their own nature as human beings, to regain control over their own humanity by becoming more self-aware, more self-correcting and hence more self-fulfilling."

Such a cultural crusade was not a popular notion for some recalcitrant Aspenites, as characterized by Elizabeth Paepcke after an incident she witnessed in 1952: "One day under the Jerome porte-cochere, I saw Luke Short, the author of popular Westerns, holding my husband by the longer end of his necktie and shaking him as one would do a dog. The more Walter struggled, the tighter grew the noose, and Walter turned purple as he gasped for air. With each shake, Short shouted: 'Stop! Walter, stop ... trying ... to ... force ... culture ... down ... the ... throats ... of ... good ... honest ... laboring ... Aspen citizens!'"

Luke Short (aka Fred Glidden) articulated a division in Aspen's community amid a clash of historic epochs. "Many Aspen locals from the mining era," said Glidden, "longed passionately to see Aspen's skies murky with the smoke of a mill or smelter, and to them, a new shaft house is a far nobler work of man than the cunning architecture of a symphony." This growing community rift was later intensified when

Paepcke declared that a rodeo not be held at the Aspen Meadows while concerts were underway in the music tent, setting off a conflict in 1954 dubbed "music vs. manure."

Paepcke unintentionally widened this community rift when, in the early 1950s, he brought in Bauhaus designer and artist Herbert Bayer to coordinate design elements for the nascent Aspen Institute campus, and also for the town. Paepcke made a gaffe that became legend when he offered free house paint to locals who would dress up their homes in colors chosen by Bayer and according to a color scheme that would make Aspen more attractive to the highbrow visitors Paepcke hoped to attract. The offer was met with sneers and denounced as a patronizing gesture from the grand pooh-bah from Chicago whose tastes were on a higher plane than this mountain town could then apprehend.

Aspen's big four in the early 1950s, each attired in Austrian garb. From left to right, Friedl Pfeifer, Walter Paepcke, Herbert Bayer and Gary Cooper. ASPEN HISTORICAL SOCIETY TED RYAN COLLECTION

A third identity in Aspen's congealing social milieu was the ski community spearheaded by a gung-ho cohort of 10th Mountain Division veterans who found common ground in Aspen just as skiing was exciting popular exuberance in the United States.

Paepcke had surmised that skiing would become a necessary attraction and cash cow, but not the centerpiece of Aspen. Skiing would furnish a pleasant distraction for visiting seminarians and, as a business, help to support the Aspen Institute's intellectual pursuits, which were foremost in his fertile mind.

However, skiing promoted a far more rapid expenditure of Aspen's social capital, as the Chicago Daily Tribune reported Feb. 11, 1954: "Aspen Confronted by Crisis; Meets It with a 'Jeep Lift':

> "Skiers and townsfolk at this famed winter resort basked today in the warmth of a community spirit that wiped out dis-

appointment for hundreds when it burst forth to offset a mechanical emergency.

The incident arose without warning. The little mountain village was a swarm with 585 skiers. The snow was at its best, the slopes in perfect condition, but the famous chairlift, longest in the world, had broken down. Replacement of a needed part would take days.

The morning sun revealed a fleet of 46 Jeeps awaiting the eager skiers assembled at a slope known as Little Nell. The Jeeps were manned by ranchers, tradesmen, lodge owners, and other residents who interrupted personal activities to help the grounded skiers. Loads of happy men and women were hauled up the road, through forest and snowfields, to the Sundeck [at the top of Aspen Mountain]. The improvised service enabled skiers to make the normal number of runs.

The whole town cooperated in helping provide the unusual service. Oil men donated tanks of oil for Jeep engines. Beer and sandwiches were carted to the scene for volunteer drivers. Skiers said they would never forget the thrill of the Jeep rides up the narrow mountain track through breathtaking scenery."

America was falling in love with skiing, thanks in part to Olympic ski stars such as Stein Eriksen and Jean-Claude Killy, who competed in international races that brought a European flare to Aspen and attracted a bevy of celebrity skiers who exuded a fetching style of outdoor glamour.

As skiing evolved, gabardine pleated slacks and Tyrolean jackets morphed into form-fitting Bogner stretch pants and tight-fitting sweaters to provide just the right contours of style. Skiing in Aspen eventually expanded onto four mountains, and winter recreation provided an ever-greater share of the Aspen economy and community identity.

Further community diversity came with those attracted like moths to Aspen's emerging brilliance—musicians, designers, Alpinists, physicists, philosophers, cyclists, authors, artists, dancers and others. Aspen's once-moribund monoculture quickly expanded into a diverse community with a complex weave that city and county land-use planners later jumbled together as "messy vitality." Within that complex mix grew competing elements that often worked at cross-purposes. However, as long as there was a perceived balance and an egalitarian inclusivity, the evolving Aspen community could attach itself to a common identity under the ephemeral and potentially overarching "Aspen Idea," the enriching unity of body, mind and spirit fomented by Paepcke and the Aspen Institute.

To Paepcke's disappointment, however, skiing was to eclipse the pursuit of high ideals and intellectual offerings. The "body" took precedence, rising head and shoulders above the "mind" and "spirit," which Aspen savants decried as a vulgar submission to hedonism. "Recreation and culture do not mix smoothly," said one critic, who observed the heady popularity of skiing in 1950 after Aspen's first Federation Internationale du Ski FIS race.

Paepcke had assumed that Aspen's cultural foundation would be anchored not on physical pleasures or on greed and luxury, but rather on the unrelenting pursuit of moral and ethical principles as keystones to participatory citizenship. Aspen's salvation would be ensured by a community consensus that championed the noble thoughts and righteous actions advanced by avatars of moral philosophy such as Wolfgang Goethe and Albert Schweitzer. Ideas would be disseminated through civil dialogue in Bauhaus-styled octagonal seminar rooms.

But the ethereal heights were beyond reach when one's feet were planted firmly on the ground. To be an aspirant to Paepcke's vision one was required to stand on the shoulders of moral and intellectual exemplars. Enlightenment required an embrace of the realm of the spirit by, according to Albert Schwietzer's mores, humbly respecting all of life and altruistically advancing humanism. All else was heedless distraction. As Goethe warned the hedonists: "A useless life is but an early death."

Consensus on the higher plateaus of life and thought were often lost to those who peaked at the earthly elevation of Aspen's lofty city limits at 7,908 feet. As multiple attractions caught on, Aspen's prestige became inceasingly materialistic, creating a tension that the Aspen Institute's resident philosopher, Mortimer Adler, observed when he pointed out that "Aspen is caught between two competing triads: the platonic—the good, the true and the beautiful; and the Machiavellian—money, fame and power."

Ever since the Quiet Years, Aspen had ruminated on the "what if" of its own success. With every commercial advance, a segment of the Aspen community reflected more on what had been lost than on what had been gained. Hindsight is always 20/20, but in Aspen, self-reflection failed to arrive at a vital and honest appraisal of incremental change. Swayed by commercial and economic interests, there has long been a willingness to move forward into ever-greater, more-ambitious promotions at risk of losing heart and soul.

Today, looking back more than 70 years, the vote for Goethe Festival II in 1950 was not a true plebiscite, but it indicated a willingness to pursue economic growth as a lasting policy. For those few who resisted monetary values and instead championed what they had referred to as the "free and easy life," well, that life had no financial bearing and was, in fact, contrary to boosting retail sales, property values and tax revenues.

Progress demanded more and better festivals, more and bigger promotions, more and broader commercialization to attract more and bigger spending guests. Progress demanded more and more of everything sellable, and that required ready access.

In the early years, getting people to Aspen in a critical mass that could enrich the resort economy was no mean feat. An airport was needed that could accommodate commercial airlines and private jets. Paved roads and four-lane highways were deemed essential for getting people from there to here and back again. Progress in Aspen became a loaded word—and still is—for portions of the community.

This emergent clash of opposing visions has, for decades, made Aspen an ideological, internecine battleground that threatens its very soul.

CHAPTER 6

Aspen: Community or Commodity?

Elitism, capitalism, the counter culture, and the new age of affluence

Aspen, the tempest in a teapot, makes a relatively small footprint in the
upper Roaring Fork Valley against the dramatic backdrop of Aspen Mountain.
This quaint grid of streets has fostered an embattled community for decades as economic,
social and cultural changes have wrought a series of identity crises,
the most current of which questions whether Aspen is a community or a commodity.
ECOFLIGHT

WHEN ELIZABETH PAEPCKE (1902-1994), in her final years, reflected on the Aspen of her dreams and the utopian visions of her husband, Walter, she conveyed an (in a speech to the Aspen Institute) outpouring of sorrow over something sacred and ethereal that she felt had been made profane.

"A good deal of courage, imagination and shared guts was needed to do such a thing in a sleepy, almost dead little town in the high Rockies," she said. "The goal was to make something better than what was begun. My sorrow now lies in the fact that people have come to Aspen to make money. My heart is broken."

Paepcke spoke from the experience of a past heartbreak when a woodland idyll she had created as a child was desecrated by a vandal. Her lament for Aspen evinced yet another ideal dashed to ruins.

Aspen scribe Peggy Clifford felt Paepcke's pain and shared her view of Aspen as precious, unique and intangible: "Aspen is more than the sum of its parts," Clifford wrote in *To Aspen and Back* (1980), her memoir about Aspen in the 1950s, '60s and '70s. "Aspen is an idea."

Today, many who find themselves in the grips of sentimental loss for a venerated past express similar laments almost daily in paeans to the local newspapers. The gradual and inevitable erosion of familiar people and places in Aspen reflects a community faced with irrevocable and often irreconcilable change.

The most-recent expressions of grief have decried the renaming of the Benedict Music Tent in exchange for a $17 million donation to the Aspen Music Festival and School, monetizing what to many is a sacred venue. Another lament mourns the renaming of Pandora's on Aspen Mountain, where lift-served skiing has made bump runs out of cherished side-country powder stashes.

To many, Aspen appears to be a commodity open to the highest bidder, a place where everything is for sale, where namesake properties are bought and sold as on a Monopoly board, where marketers, real estate agents, appraisers, speculators, bankers and economists are castigated for knowing the price of everything and the value of nothing.

In Aspen today, community members gather for wakes and memorials where they feel a disappearing community bond. Aspen churches and schools remain bastions of community for parents and their children, even though few of those children will have the option to buy in and live in Aspen as working adults. Affordable worker housing in Aspen has enormous demand, and lotteries offer the chance that winners may live in a worker enclave rather than integrating the social strata with what community planners have long referred to as "messy vitality."

It used to be that ZG license plates, 81612 and 81611 ZIP codes, the 925 telephone prefix and Aspen's 7,908-foot elevation identified true locals. Now, it's an address in Woody Creek, Basalt, El Jebel, Missouri Heights, Blue Lake, Carbondale and beyond.

The incursions of land developers and speculators in Aspen and Pitkin County are seen in massive vacation homes that belie the esoteric heritage of Aspen's non-materialistic cultural roots, which sprouted in 1949 with the Goethe Bicentennial. Aspen's embattled community, especially where housing is concerned, is conflicted by the feckless commoditization that has driven out of much of the local workforce, much of which now commutes long distances to service extravagant properties.

Author Saul Bellow, who spent time in Aspen as a visitor in the 1960s, and witnessed gentrifying trends, suggested that Aspen risked becoming a "pleasure slum."

WELCOME TO THE KULTURSTAAT

ELIZABETH PAEPCKE HAD FOUND elation in the potential for Aspen to thrive under a magical spell manifested by her husband's original vision of an idealized "kulturstaat," or culture state, a "high-minded" community that would honor and protect what nature and historical circumstance had wondrously preserved since the mining era.

"Here in the heart of the most materialistic nation in the history of humankind," Peggy Clifford romanticized, "was a town so bent on responding in another way to the imperatives of the times that it built its economy on classical music, scholarly debates and snow."

During the brief 15 years of his influence in Aspen, Walter Paepcke had become a kind of gatekeeper who vowed to keep the rabble at bay in deference to a lofty, intellectual, nonmaterialistic lifestyle. Part of that formula required exclusivity, as Paepcke and friends displayed at the Four Seasons Club in the 1950s.

Hal Rothman, in his 1998 book *Devil's Bargains*, described "a private club for Paepcke's associates with plans to designate private fishing rights along Castle Creek and infuse the club with an elitist, urbane overlay that burned locals with resentment."

Rothman might have been writing about contemporary Aspen's exclusivity when he characterized Paepcke's vision for Aspen. Rather than lionize the Chicago industrialist, Rothman described the unintended consequences of a kulturstaat where "Paepcke's friends and associates began the trend of building luxury second homes, changing the topography and demography of the town incrementally."

Paepcke's ambition to make Aspen "a center for understanding and ideas and of transmitting values and meaning in a rapidly changing time," wrote Rothman, was synchronistic with a national, societal shift. "Paepcke's experiment in idiosyncratic enlightened capitalism proved to be a pivotal moment in the evolution of tourism in the 20th-century West, a bridge between a more elitist past and a future of mass culture."

By 1959, reported Rothman, more than 200 second-home owners were added to the community's 1,800 full-time residents. In Aspen today, 45% of the city's housing stock, tabulated in a 2021 report as over 2,600 units, consists of units not occupied by a full-time resident. "Aspen acquired a year-round economy and the associated activities that would only grow over time," wrote Rothman. "Meanwhile, Aspen had a ripple effect on Basalt, where vacationing fishermen began coveting river frontage and parceling out the prime holes."

The downvalley ripple of Aspen's regional influence became pronounced in the 1960s when a group of Aspen vigilantes took chain saws to Highway 82 billboards they deemed obnoxious blights on the rural landscape. Others sought to protect the upper Roaring Fork Valley through legislative action.

In 1955, Aspen's first zoning ordinance was passed to address the rising demand for development: Tourist accommodations could be built only in areas where such facilities already existed; construction in Aspen's West End had to be on lots equally spacious to the large lots there; and businesses were restricted to the four-block historic business district. These rudimentary guidelines positioned Aspen to become one of the most costly places to build with one of the most restrictive land-use codes in the United States.

A madcap event in the mid-1960s, the Snowmass Ski Splash drew thousands of spectators to witness people doing crazy things on skis, most of them ending with a splash in an outdoor pool. Such was the exuberance of skiing as its popularity grew and the ski mystique attracted a burgeoning industry to the upper Roaring Fork Valley.
ASPEN HISTORICAL SOCIETY

WHEN ASPEN 'SPLIT WIDE OPEN'

IN 1960, Walter Paepcke was fatally stricken with bone and lung cancer. Aspen's thought leader and cultural icon died April 13, 1960, at age 61. "When Arco oilman R.O. Anderson assumed the [Aspen] Institute's leadership," wrote Rothman, "Paepcke's hegemony was all but removed, as was the sway he had held with Aspen old-timers who were gradually voted out of offices they and their forebears had held since the mining years. Aspen lost part of its rudder, and politics became competitive and contentious."

"The place split wide open," Clifford wrote of Aspen in the 1960s. "A kind of anarchy surfaced. It had become a free-for-all. Fundamental questions had been left unraised and left unanswered. Nothing was guiding Aspen now but its own momentum."

That momentum was largely driven by what Rothman described as "neonatives," a new and often-transitory breed of "locals" who laid claim to Aspen. Young people had "all come to look for America," as Paul Simon and Art Garfunkel harmonized, and Aspen became hallowed ground in that generational search.

When Clifford arrived in Aspen in the early 1960s, she befriended Fred Glidden, an Aspen writer of Western novels whose pen name was Luke Short. "You will like Aspen," Glidden told Clifford. "It is a fine, quirky place. There are people here who are straight out of Fitzgerald—golden people whose appetites are as extraordinary as their charms. They play hard and work hard and have no conventional ambitions."

Clifford described a unique place and time in what seemed like a once-in-a-lifetime alignment of the planets: "We were a special and consecrated breed inhabiting the best of all possible worlds, unspoiled by excess, spacious, open and tranquil. We wore our voluntary poverty like a medal and boasted of our moral superiority."

Aspen's isolation, natural beauty and lack of pretension provided fertile ground for the counterculture movement of the 1960s and '70s, when a surging flood of American youths broke from the mainstream and defined a liberal lifestyle like none before. "People look at Aspen as a refuge," said one resident in 1970, "a place where you can live the way you want to live, do your own thing in a creative way, and it's accepted."

However, a core of Aspen's old guard was not at all accepting. They derided the hip, young intruders who invaded their so-called paradise. Guido Meyer, Aspen's magistrate, became consumed by a personal vendetta against hippies, and he dispensed a punitive form of justice upon those whom he considered threats to the decency of his community of friends and neighbors. A selection of Guido's quotes, published by Aspen Illustrated News, a precursor to the *Aspen Daily News*, reveals the unmasked hostility of Aspen's foremost police authority:

"Beatniks, hippies, they all have long hair. That's how I can tell them. I prefer dogs to hippies. Dogs are cleaner and have more manners."

"Hippies are supported by communists. They are working from within. It's the same as the Third Column in the '30s that gave rise to Hitler."

"Riots, hippies, beatniks. They are all the same; working from Moscow. Lawlessness and disorder will be our downfall."

"We have gotten too weak. We are not tough like we were in the old days when we took care of the cattle thieves."

Nonetheless, a revolution was underway in Aspen that shattered the community solidarity that had marked the Quiet Years. A young Aspen attorney named Joe Edwards, who would later profoundly influence Aspen as a county commissioner, took Guido and his minions to task and challenged their conservative, authoritarian dictates based on the contemporaneous groundswell of the Civil Rights Movement. The "hippie trials" proved a successful crusade that would eventually expel the old guard and replace it with a new and ambitious generation of local leaders who would take Aspen into a more liberal era.

Around this time, Aspen's first master plan—the Aspen Area General Plan—was created in 1966. The plan—initiated by Bauhaus designer Herbert Bayer, 10th Mountain Division veteran and architect Fritz Benedict, and Glidden—would manage rapid growth as seen during the previous decade when, between 1950 and 1960, Aspen's population increased 44.7%. Another, even-larger jump occurred be- tween 1960 and 1970, when Aspen's population exploded 158%.

At the time of the master plan, Aspen's population was 2,300, with another 1,000 outlying in rural Pitkin County, plus accommodations for 6,000 visitors. The plan's stated purpose was "to retain the fine balance between man and his environment, the essence of Aspen's character." Among recommendations was a light-rail system between Aspen and Snowmass, which would later be sidetracked by four-laning Highway 82, a contentious issue that fostered a decades long debate that carries on today.

"The master plan became our bible, our Declaration of Independence," extolled Clifford. "The rebels liked it because it ensured controlled growth. The burghers liked it because it ensured orderly growth—the sort that affluent America would approve of, the sort that would keep the rabble out and keep prices up." Clifford, who would flee Aspen in the late 1970s after her passionate love affair with the town and community soured, ruefully noted a telltale advertisement in the *New York Times*: "Aspen is a party and you're invited."

SNOWMASS AND CONDO BONDAGE

WHEN THE SNOWMASS ski resort was developed in 1967-68, it ushered in what Rothman termed "group think" and "a purely capitalistic economic model that ushered in the era of the condominium." He added: "The very construction of condominiums diminished the distinctions between neo-native and local. The social reconfiguration of the community matched its physical changes, depriving the older Aspen of powerful community leadership at the moment it needed it most."

The Snowmass Mall in the late 1960s. The family-oriented ski resort was completed just in time for the winter ski season of 1967-68. ASPEN HISTORICAL SOCIETY

"One could buy a condominium," observed Clifford, "use it several times a year, rent it short term for the rest of the year, apply the rental income to the purchase price, and write off most expenses courtesy of the IRS while the condo appreciated rapidly in value." The era of the traditional family lodge was ending.

Aspen soon experienced a phenomenal resort boom in which wealth became the hallmark of a high-altitude playground that harked back to the opulence of the silver barons. With the boom came the lucrative potential for growth and development that pitted factions against one another in a passionate struggle to define Aspen. Rather than guarding only against external economic forces, Aspen had to confront internal agents of self-interest in an internecine struggle that pitted idealism against economics and slow-growthers against full-steam-ahead capitalists.

"The locals liked the town the way it was," Clifford observed in 1970, "a natural fortress of light and air and green and good smells. The dudes saw that sweet fortress as a bonanza and set about to mine its riches."

"Between 1960 and 1965," reported Rothman, "Aspen's population rose by more than 40%, most people coming for the combination of ambience and skiing. Included in this group were journalist Hunter S. Thompson and his wife, Sandy. Of all groups, these 'newest-comers' were the least enthusiastic about the increasingly corporate structure of the ski company and about the very growth of which they were part. They embraced a mythic Aspen, one that probably never existed, but they were sure that their efforts to save the community were right. They also saw protest about change as an entry into local society, a way to prove their right to local, or at least to neonative, status, paradoxically by closing the doors behind them."

Aspen developer Hans Cantrup (left) and Aspen Institute Board Chairman Robert O. Anderson made a deal in 1980 to sell the Institute's holdings at the Aspen Meadows cultural campus for $6 million. This sale signaled a divorce between the Institute and Aspen that was finally reconciled in 1992, when the Aspen Meadows Consortium, a broad-based group of community-minded Aspenites, reinstated the Institute's ownership for a resale price of $10.
ASPEN HISTORICAL SOCIETY ASPEN TIMES COLLECTION

ASPEN GOES ALL AGLITTER

WHEN 20TH CENTURY FOX bought the Aspen Skiing Co. in 1978, ending the era of local ownership, Aspen skiing became fully commoditized. Aspen's fault lines widened as the city proceeded toward a vague and troubled destiny in which everyone was complicit. "We are all industrial tourists," Rothman wrote. "Physically, we can take only pictures and leave only footprints. Psychically, socially,

Hunter S. Thompson, the regaled gonzo journalist, made the Aspen area his home in the mid-1960s when the community faced tumultuous social and cultural upheavals. Thompson's presence helped to radicalize Aspen's image, especially in 1969 and 1970, when he ran for sheriff in a highly contentious election that pitted Aspen's conservative old guard against a new and liberal young population. Thompson lost his bid for sheriff, but a new order came to define Aspen as a bastion of liberalism with a hip party town atmosphere. ASPEN HISTORICAL SOCIETY KRUEGER COLLECTION

culturally, economically and environmentally, we inexorably change all we touch."

Today, Aspen's liberal fringe temperament has lost some of its formative fervor as escalated property values have pushed much of the local workforce downvalley and diffused the political influences of those who had been Aspen's radical advocates. The downvalley exodus was, in part, an unintentional result of growth restrictions legislated to control the sprawl that had threatened Aspen's small-town authenticity. Rapid gentrification alienated the more humble elements of the upper valley's once-divergent population, leaving large neighborhoods mostly vacant during off-seasons, when second-home owners take up residences elsewhere.

Aspen's hallowed Shangri-La attracted the super-rich like bees to honey and, despite aggressive subsidized-housing measures, moved the workforce out. Traffic jams clogged the streets and highways as private jets clogged the skies. Contention over political and land-use issues fueled perpetual vitriolic debate as conspicuous consumption and revelry redefined the Aspen image.

In 1976, Anderson, Walter Paepcke's successor as board chair at the Aspen Institute, warned, "The popular image of a fun-oriented, anything-goes town may not be consistent with an organization which is trying to deal with major problems in a serious manner ... Imagine trying to run a major university in downtown Las Vegas."

By the late 1970s, the kulturstaat that Paepcke had envisioned found purity only in the cloistered sanctuary of the Aspen Meadows campus, the so-called "Circle of Serenity." Even that bastion was under siege when, in 1980, the Aspen Institute, under Anderson's leadership, spurned Aspen by selling its Meadows properties to local developer Hans Cantrup for $6 million. This led to a succession of developers as Cantrup lost his holdings through foreclosure to John Roberts, who in turn lost the property through another foreclosure, in 1984, to developer Mohammed Hadid and moneyman Sheik Al Ibrahim, brother-in-law of Saudi Arabia's King Fahd. Donald Trump was at one time a bidder on these and other Aspen properties.

The institute held a 90-year lease, but a divorce was imminent as the institute and Aspen suffered seemingly irreconcilable differences in a dramatic community rift when the city thwarted the institute's rezoning plans to develop a large hotel. After protracted dialogue and pained diplomacy, the divorce was reconciled in 1992, when the Aspen Meadows Consortium, a broad-based group of community-minded Aspenites, reinstated the institute's ownership for a resale price of $10 (that's right—$10!), constituting a generous donation from Al Ibrahim that reassured the institute's place in Aspen's cultural community.

John Sarpa, today an independent developer and community-minded businessman, came to Aspen in 1984 to navigate Aspen's land-use labyrinth with Hadid and Al Ibrahim. Sarpa was instrumental in hammering out the hard-won resolution: "I was honored to be a co-chair of the Aspen Meadows Consortium, as we were able to find that elusive balance of private, local nonprofit and community interests for the long-term cultural benefit of Aspen."

Aspen and the institute eventually made peace, but only when both parties realized the value of the other and made amends to live peaceably, if somewhat apart. But the split with Paepcke's ideals was never rejoined. The institute dropped "Humanistic Studies" from its title, embracing ambitious "thought leading to action" policy-oriented programs that have become global in scope.

James Sloan Allen wrote that the split between town and gown was only one more schism in an overall abandonment of Paepcke's original humanistic idealism. "Aspen and the institute were swept up in historic currents that brought the transition from industrial to postindustrial society, from a self-denying to a self-centered character type, and from modernist to postmodernist culture," wrote Allen. "The history of Aspen is thus the history of American culture at the mid-century and

This time-lapse image in 2019 at the Aspen airport illustrates the intensity of jet traffic over an eight-hour period on a single day in which 290 flights came and went to Aspen.
PETE MCBRIDE

after." Aspen came to define what Allen termed "the culture of narcissism."

Perhaps no one personified narcissism in Aspen more fully than a New York developer named Donald Trump, who descended upon Aspen in 1984 to bid on another of Roberts' foreclosures. During one of Trump's ski trips here in 1989 with then-wife Ivana, an alleged affair with a woman who would become Trump's second wife, 26-year-old model Marla Maples, caused a stir outside Bonnie's Restaurant on Aspen Mountain when Ivana confronted the paramours in a public display of contretemps.

Tawdry scandals aside, the fracturing of the Aspen community accelerated in a whirlwind of real estate excitements that engendered land-use controversies, a prominent one being the development of a five-star Ritz Carlton hotel (today's St. Regis), which was completed in 1992.

Despite the soul-aching infighting, Aspen's most unifying commonality has long been its enduring and inspiring physical setting. Today, an echo of Paepcke's Aspen Idea— a place that nurtures body, mind and spirit—beckons to close the gap between divergent worldviews in a setting everyone can agree is an aesthetic ideal. Aspenites may not agree on politics and land use, but most agree that the Elk Mountains are stunningly beautiful. However, mutual respect for the mountains does not presuppose agreement on how to live in them. Thus, a host of ongoing upheavals have conspired to overwhelm the essence of Aspen's cherished mountain vibe. Corporeal desires and distractions have come to hold sway over loftier goals and sentiments as, for many, the "body" of the Aspen Idea has taken prominence over "mind" and "spirit."

Profitability through tourism—what Paepcke had advocated in moderation—has now long been the driving force for the burgeoning resort, where a profligate playground frivolity has all but overshadowed scholarly and artistic pursuits with spectacles such as the X Games, Gay Ski Week, Food & Wine, snow polo and other activities that cater to mass entertainments. In a partying atmosphere of contagious diversions, the triad at the heart of the Aspen Idea has wobbled out of balance. Robert Maynard Hutchins long ago moralized on this impasse of values: "I can never get over the notion that having fun is a form of indolence."

The construction of the Ritz Carlton lodging project, today's St. Regis, is shown in 1991. The hotel's development marked an acceleration in a whirlwind of real estate excitements that engendered land-use controversies. ASPEN HISTORICAL SOCIETY ASPEN TIMES COLLECTION

The spell that had hidden Brigadoon in the mists of time was broken. Paepcke's cloistered ideal was overrun by commercialism and the objectification of Aspen. The city retains the rich cultural vestiges of Paepcke's dream—music, art and philosophy—for those who can afford the cover charge, but idealism was doomed. Utopia was a field of dreams. Machiavelli was put in charge of the venue, as Mortimer Adler had reckoned long ago.

THE "SUPERGENTRIFICATION" OF ASPEN

TODAY, the struggle for community ensues as diverse constituencies attempt to shape and mold Aspen in their own image. This ongoing battle of influences makes for a thriving political, social and cultural exchange. The debate, however, is often divisive as competing community factions vie for a share of paradise. Aspen's volatile, argumentative soul-searching evinces an energetic fervor in debating the contrasting values that divide Aspenites with a hotly articulated sense of ownership that is especially active during times of intense change. And in Aspen, change is the only constant.

Consider lift-ticket prices, which have plotted an irreversible upward trend since the "Boat Tow" cost skiers a dime per ride. During the 2023-24 ski season, SkiCo charged $244 for a single-day lift ticket, which was still surprisingly competitive with Vail Resorts' single-day window price of $299. Another constant, of course, is the steep climb of Aspen real estate prices into the nosebleed altitudes.

In her 2021 book, *Aspen and the American Dream: How One Town Manages Inequality in the Era of Supergentrification*, sociologist Jenny Stuber pinpoints Aspen's social-engineering challenge of guiding development as described by a city planning goal: "a process of place-making that involves the careful orchestration of diverse class interests within local politics and the community, with the overarching goal of maintaining Aspen's value and preserving its authentic small-town character."

Many agree that Aspen's small-town character is on life-support, a casualty of the supergentrification that has made Aspen a social and economic anomaly: "The conventional wisdom," writes Stuber, "is that a place like Aspen should not exist. That is, a place should not exist where the median income is $73,000 per year, but the median home price is over $10 million . . . These dynamics should make it impossible for a community to exist where the incomes earned by local residents are fundamentally at odds with the housing prices, and where working locals still exert considerable influence on how the town operates."

Working-class Aspenites have struggled long and hard to keep up against long odds. When ski patrollers organized and went on strike for higher wages in the '70s and '80s, a picket sign at the newly installed Silver Queen gondola in 1986 read: "SkiCo got the Silver Queen. We got the shaft." Other beachhead controversies have kept passions inflamed: the four-laning of Highway 82, the Ritz-Carlton and Little Nell hotels, the private Caribou Club, a proposed ban on fur coats, Prince Bandar's 55,000-square-foot monster home, airport expansions, the Lift One Gorsuch kerfuffle, outrageous displays such as Champagne-spraying debauches at Cloud Nine, and the opulent excess of Aspen X.

Stuber accurately describes the perpetual growth mandate that has driven Aspen for more than five decades: "A pro-growth agenda is pushed by economic elites and government officials who seek to maximize the exchange value of a place—its economic value in terms of how much it can be rented or sold for . . . Yet local residents are typically no match for the growth machine, which benefits from the deep pockets and continuous, institutionalized support of local political regimes."

Stuber writes that Aspen currently caters to those "with upscale global tastes." What makes the place attractive, she infers, is a tantalizing blend of historic, homespun Colorado mountain chic and urbane corporeal and cultural pleasures. The community, she opines, is "co-opted by economic elites and a 'butler class' of professionals—lawyers, accountants, politicians and more . . . who help them achieve their goals." These goals are clearly visible in conspicuous consumption and conspicuous waste—two societal sins in Thorstein Veblen's lampoon, *The Theory of the Leisure Class*, in which Aspen could be a case study.

"Aspen is a rare town," said Ann Bond, a consulting curator from the State Historical Society, "in that it has a solid history of boom and bust, as well as a wide range of industrial and commer-

The Gorsuch brand in Aspen was tarnished when, operating under the name Norway Island LLC, an entity connected to Jeff Gorsuch of Aspen in July 2021 paid $10 million for nearly one acre of land at the base Aspen Mountain, land for which the group three years prior won voter approval to build the future Gorsuch Haus commercial and lodging development. In 2022, the same property was flipped for $76.25 million when Norway Island sold it to an LLC controlled by Miami-based OKO Group, run by Russian-born billionaire Vladislav Doronin. The Gorsuch logo ("Gorsucks") was altered by an unknown artist in protest against blatant profiteering and a public campaign that had garnered electoral support for the development by identifying it with an Aspen family brand.
PAUL ANDERSEN/ASPEN JOURNALISM

cial development through its history. However, the defining attribute of Aspen in the last 40 years has been its role as one of few internationally famed resort/living communities for the extremely wealthy of the entire world. This quality of the town is so pervasive that it is visible always."

A local columnist emoted in the *Aspen Daily News* that Aspen is no longer a true ski town: "Aspen is a corporate town replete with middle managers. Aspen is a town where the hyper-wealthy can go mental on hedonism. Aspen is a town where absentee landlords can mine money while giving absolutely nothing back. Aspen is a shopping town, an upscale mall. Aspen is a bedroom community where nobody lives in the bedrooms."

"The lessons of the Western past appear in complex layers in the Roaring Fork Valley," observed University of Colorado Boulder history professor and author Patricia Limerick. "From the impermanence of the traditional extractive economy to the benefits and costs of the contemporary tourist economy, understanding Aspen means understanding crucial regional issues."

A DEVASTATING FUTURE, OR A MODEL OF EXCELLENCE?

IN A 1999 speech to the Aspen Institute Society of Fellows, Aspen Mayor John Bennett, who served from 1991 to 1999, pointed out emergent regional concerns. In 1991, he said, the Roaring Fork region had a population of 48,000. By 1998, that number had grown to about 60,000. "The new people moving here in the next decade will make an extra 120,000 automobile trips per day in our valley," Bennett accurately predicted. "Our Roaring Fork region's underlying zoning today will allow a total build-out of 300,000 people. The impact of such growth on our environment and quality of life would be devastating."

Bennett warned that arguing over opposing values has threatened a breakdown of civility. "We are in danger of succumbing to a politics of division and anger, an anger that is reflected in letters-to-the-editor in any given week," he said. "Indeed, the shrillness of uncivil dialogue appears to grow almost monthly, with big-city accusations of fraud, patronage, lying and general malfeasance on the part of anyone in public office. For some of our citizens, engaging in an honest and open dialogue with neighbors in a small town has been replaced by sitting at home, alone, with a word processor, and firing off ugly emails to the local newspapers. Aspen has become a political battleground."

This ugly tone, said Bennett, threatens to tarnish "a city which has celebrated the life of the mind, a place of the arts in the human experience, the politics of class, the fine-tuning of the body through mountain sports, the values of rural living, and a vibrant and contagious youthfulness."

Spectacles such as the X Games, shown here in January 2023, illustrate how profitability through tourism—what Paepcke had advocated in moderation—grew into a driving force for the burgeoning resort, where a profligate playground frivolity has all but overshadowed scholarly and artistic pursuits. AUSTIN COLBERT/THE ASPEN TIMES

Bennett offered a way out: "Our role is to provide a model for excellence, not merely for being a wealthy town in a beautiful place, but a model of civilization in a small community. We can offer the world a model of a community consciously founded on a vision and a dream. We owe it to our founders—but far more important, we owe it to ourselves—to live up to that dream."

CHAPTER 7

Community Blossoms Along the Colorado River

'Better jobs, closer to home'
reshapes the region

Colorado Drifters is all about community gatherings in New Castle, where there is a "Pay it Forward" board for those who need something on the run and leave an IOU. Alicia Gresley pays as she goes at the cash register.

PAUL ANDERSEN/ASPEN JOURNALISM

As workers from the Aspen community have incrementally been pushed downvalley over the decades by a tsunami of surging real estate prices and an erosion of accessible housing, seeds of community have taken root elsewhere, finding niches in which to blossom.

These communities may be little known to much of the upper Roaring Fork Valley, but for workers who make its economy hum, it's where they own homes, raise families, build dreams, struggle with life, and rush back and forth for employment each workday on congested highways. These communities are humble, mostly affordable, individuated by their unique characters, and yet cohesive in their diversity. Few second homes or short-term rentals erode neighborhoods that are alive with families invested there.

It was to three of these communities—New Castle, Silt and Rifle—I traveled, taking a Roaring Fork Transportation Authority (RFTA) bus to the end of the line in a search of thriving communities and new economic prospects.

These communities house much of the upper Roaring Fork Valley workforce, commuters who may one day choose "better jobs, closer to home," which is the tagline of an economic development initiative that may dramatically change patterns of commerce and culture throughout the region.

At 7:15 a.m. on a weekday, I climbed aboard the big blue bus in Basalt to start my day-long field trip. I was surprised to find more than a dozen passengers, most of whom were sleeping in the dim half-light of a January morning—the night shift on their way home.

The bus picked up speed down Two Rivers Road where the driver swerved around a small herd of mule deer. Going against a flood of upvalley commuters in a double flow of headlights, we soon reached the 27th Street transfer station in Glenwood Springs, where the Grand Hogback bus loaded and maneuvered us down Grand Avenue.

Downtown New Castle on a quiet winter morning reveals the town's rural appeal and opportunities for economic development.
PAUL ANDERSEN/ASPEN JOURNALISM

Merging onto Interstate 70 in West Glenwood, the bus motored 10 miles west to the New Castle exit. I got off at the downtown stop on an empty, quiet street with low storefronts stretching in both directions. As the bus pulled away, I realized I had stepped into rural western Colorado.

Alicia Gresley was to be my guide. She called and apologized for being late, explaining that she was held up by a highway wreck slowing traffic on the drive from her home in Rifle, where she serves on the City Council. Gresley also heads up the Colorado River Valley Economic Development Partnership, a nonprofit that assists existing small businesses and encourages new businesses to locate in western Garfield County. The idea, she later explained, is to provide smart growth opportunities for entrepreneurs and generate new options for local workers who call the Colorado River Valley home.

Gresley is energetic, a perfect fit for her role. She said that "Better jobs, closer to home" is a slogan that signals a potential shift in the regional workforce. If Gresley is successful, workers will have greater choice between the commuter rigors of Highway 82 and a diversity of local jobs in communities where most of them live. This could portend a boon for Colorado River communities and a challenge to the high-demand service economy of Aspen and Snowmass Village.

Gresley took me to Colorado Drifters Coffee and Fly Fishing, a quaint New Castle coffee shop run by Kyla Hemelt, who has created a warm, homey ambiance of welcoming smiles, reasonable pricing and a laid-back atmosphere that eschews attitude or pretense. The cafe doubles as a fishing and fly shop, reflecting Hemelt's love for the Colorado River, on the banks of which she lives with her husband and their two young

PARENTS AND KIDS WELCOME

HEMELT OPENED DRIFTERS in the summer of 2021, after she and her family moved from Golden, Colorado where Hemelt had been a school teacher for 14 years. "I grew up in Gunnison," she said, "and wanted to get back to the Western Slope for the river lifestyle and the small-town vibe for my family."

Alicia Gresley is a dynamic force for communities along the Colorado River. She is a town councilmember in Rifle.
PAUL ANDERSEN/ASPEN JOURNALISM

Drifters is all about community, a place to gather. "When we moved here," recalled Hemelt, "there were no coffee shops, no fly shops. There really wasn't much. This space was vacant for about two years, and multiple spaces were empty up and down the street. We had this crazy idea to start a business with no business background."

Hemelt had envisioned a business plan with another partner, whom she bought out in six months. "I was really nervous about how we would be received here because there is this old-school mentality about keeping things the way they are and not wanting change," she said. "Overall, we've been very welcomed. People are extremely friendly, and the younger families really want a place to go and bring their kids and be social and not drive to other towns."

"We have a gazillion events," said Hemelt, whose fly shop doubles as a toy room where kids play while parents gather and chat. "I'm kind of a party planner as well." There are open-mic nights mostly featuring local artists. Trivia nights, held twice a month, always have a waiting list. Drifters has become a hub that spawns a homespun, family-oriented community.

Before dropping in at New Castle Town Hall, Gresley described her origins in Perth, Australia. Her dual U.S. citizenship comes from her American father, who was a Seabee in the U.S. Navy stationed in northwest Australia, where he met Gresley's Australian mother. In 2005, on her third trip to the United States as a young backpacker, Gresley rode Amtrak to Glenwood Springs and decided to stay in the region. She landed a job at Vail that included housing. She worked winters for Vail Resorts and summers for a rafting company. Gresley eventually created her own role doing business development for the lodging sector in Eagle County where she worked to increase the number of second-home owners offering their properties as short-term vacation rentals.

Ten years after settling in Colorado, she met her husband, who grew up in Basalt. The couple moved to Rifle where they are raising two children.

"For two years, I did the commute to Avon," said Gresley, "every day, five days a week. The pandemic made me work remotely from home, which had a silver lining: I was able to spend time with my first child. It was then I became more connected to the Rifle community and wanted to get more involved."

Kyla Hemelt of Colorado Drifters is an avid fisherwoman and paddle boarder.
KYLA HEMELT PHOTOGRAPHY

Gresley ran for council and won a seat in 2021. "I wanted to be a voice for families like us," she said. "Now I really appreciate what goes into running a town in a small community."

Leaving her job in Avon—and the commute—in 2022, Gresley has dedicated herself to local government and economic growth, for which she demonstrates a deep passion. She also created her own consulting business, On Mountain Time, which she calls a *state of mind*. "Time is our most precious resource," she said, "and it's finite, especially when we spend a lot of time working for somebody else.

"My first goal is to provide resources for small businesses, especially women-run businesses. I found that, during the pandemic, a lot of women had to get creative, many having been laid off and doing home schooling. Many women I talked to started up businesses to earn an income for their families. They had a passion but didn't have the business side of it. How do you turn something that you're good at into a business and make it work?"

This is where Gresley shines.

THE VIEW FROM NEW CASTLE

WE CONTINUED TO TOWN HALL where we met Dave Reynolds, New Castle's town administrator, and Reynolds' assistant, Rochelle Firth. Reynolds has lived in New Castle for seven years and has been in his job for six, a role that enlivened a personal mission to build community.

"When I came to this area, I searched up and down 82 and I-70, and I wound up here and just fell in love with it right away," he said. "It just felt like a family community where you would be happy to raise kids."

As town administrator, Reynolds is compelled to maintain the attractive first impression that persuaded him to make his home here.

"Our intention is in giving back to our community and keeping this a comfortable place where people can raise their families," he said. "We recognize that we have a certain charm and character, and our goal is to maintain that. What we care about here is keeping that family lifestyle, that charm we have.

"Most people have only the I-70 view of New Castle, and they don't realize that we're a town of about 5,200, with about 1,500 households. These are primary homes with families, with people raising their kiddos, and it's a great place to do it."

Community is fostered in New Castle in part by an active social calendar put together by an ambitious recreation department. "We have a full year of events," Reynolds said, "and sports go year-round. And we're doing it in cooperation with our neighbors, so our leagues include towns from up and down the valley, and from outside the valley. We have arts, crafts and enrichment programs that are held almost every day."

Such positive energy pulls in families and attracts outside interest. "We have open tracts of land owned by developers who are interested in bringing in more housing," Reynolds said. "Growth is not our goal, but we know it is inevitable, and we accept it, but the goal is to maintain our charm. People pick this fun little place to live, where the parks, the trails and the schools are amazing."

Spread out north of Main Street are quiet, attractive neighborhoods connected to town by an extensive trail system that includes single-track mountain bike and hiking trails and cross-country skiing. Farther north are bucolic valleys where creeks flow down from the Flat Tops, the second-largest designated wilderness area in Colorado, at 235,214 acres. Main Elk Creek is home to limestone sport-climbing crags that have helped put this region on the international climber's map.

Like much of the Colorado River Valley, New Castle has grown significantly over the past two decades. The town's population grew from about 2,000 residents in 2000 to 4,518 in 2010 and 4,923 in 2020, according to the U.S. Census, while the number of housing units followed a similar trajectory, increasing from 746 in 2000 to 1,893 in 2020. Commercial developments include the 18-hole Lakota Canyon Golf Course, which opened for play in 2004. The area is rich with small-town character and the likelihood of continued residential growth.

"I grew up here," said Firth, "and now I live in Parachute, a 45-minute commute. Coming back here, you go to the grocery store and everyone knows you. I love it here for the small-town charm. The mayor and council are at every event. They are involved."

Reynolds said he appreciates a sense of regionalism that links the Colorado River Valley through collaborative-minded municipalities.

"We have a relationship with our neighbors that has formed between town administrators and mayors," he said. "We need to know each other so that when we have issues, we can work through them together. We are deliberate about knowing each other, and that is something that has changed in just the last decade.

"We realize that a lot of our residents don't work here, but when they get off that exit, we want them to feel like they are at home. I don't think we're ever going to get rid of the commute, but we hope to give people more options. We already have a large segment who work from their homes, which is COVID-driven, and that's a huge step in that direction."

Quiet, unpretentious and fully local, New Castle personifies rural western Colorado. Reynolds vows to work to keep it that way. "Our staff is amazing," he said, "and our mayor and Town Council take the approach of 'residents first' and of maintaining who we are. Change is inevitable, but through that, we've got to maintain who we are."

WHEN COAL WAS KING

ALMOST A CENTURY AND A HALF AGO, early Anglo settlers discovered New Castle. Prospectors and miners arrived in the early 1880s and found rich coal veins near Elk Creek's confluence with the Colorado River. The city thrived on mining, and merchants made their livings catering to miners' needs and desires. The town grew, with restaurants, grocery stores, drug stores, opera houses and hotels. At one point, the town had 22 saloons. West of Elk Creek was an area of ill repute discreetly referred to as the "Peach Orchard."

The founding father of New Castle was Jasper Ward, a freighter and farmer who was one of the town's first settlers. Ward and his family built a one-room, dirt-floor cabin along the west bank of Elk Creek. The cabin became the town's first post office and Ward the first postmaster. Ute Indian Chief Colorow was a friend who often visited Ward's cabin.

Ward later served as the town's deputy sheriff and, in August 1887, joined a unit of the Colorado National Guard that was intent on warring with some of Colorow's followers. Ward rode to the scene of the battle with the intention of brokering a peace, but as he rode toward the gathered Utes, a guardsman fired a shot that started the battle. Ward was killed in the melee. He was 37.

First known as Grand Buttes and later Chapman, the town was

incorporated as New Castle on Feb. 2, 1888. British coal miners suggested the name in reference to Newcastle-upon-Tyne, an English town noted for its coal mines. The Consolidated Mine operated just west of downtown on Ward's Peak (now Burning Mountain) and the Vulcan Mine, to the southeast, on Roderick's Ridge, across what was then called the Grand River (now the Colorado River).

New Castle became center stage for labor strikes by coal miners in protest against subhuman working conditions in unsafe mines where accidents, many of them crippling or lethal, were commonplace. One strike, in October 1893, targeted the Vulcan Mine for failure to deliver the meager wages on which miners existed. Several safety demands were coupled with the pay grievance. Conditions improved, but at the nearby Consolidated Mine, owned by Colorado Fuel & Iron (CF&I), miners stayed out for five months.

The long strike strained CF&I, but it hurt the miners more as they survived on scant savings and labor-union allowances. The superintendent had the mine boarded up and threatened to let it fill with water if the miners didn't capitulate. In time, they did, for a lower wage than before and with less than half the workforce rehired. With this precedent, the Vulcan Mine also lowered its wages to match CF&I.

The United Mine Workers (UMW) moved in to bolster the rights of the miners and called another strike. This time there was violence. A bridge of the Colorado Midland Railroad was burned to block the threatened arrival of 30 U.S. Marshals called in to quell the strike. This prompted the governor to call up the state militia to protect the trains.

The strike finally ended, but CF&I president John Osgood, the man who had built a model coal mine and coke-oven operation at Redstone, announced that his mine would be closed indefinitely. The Vulcan reopened, but in the aftermath of the strike, the miners eventually reverted to the low pay that had helped initiate the dispute. At that point, CF&I reopened its mine to a more compliant group of workers. By 1896, New Castle held the lion's share of coal mining in Garfield County, with 287 miners working coal seams.

The Vulcan became notorious for an explosion that ripped through its tunnels on Feb. 18, 1896. Mine timbers were reportedly

New Castle Town Administrator Dave Reynolds and assistant Rochelle Firth.
PAUL ANDERSEN/ASPEN JOURNALISM

blown 400 feet from the mouth of the mine and into the Colorado River. Body-recovery efforts took three weeks. The explosion killed 49 men. A total of 37 children lost their fathers that day. The Vulcan was soon closed and flooded.

In 1899, Osgood's Consolidated Mine caught fire. Despite efforts to douse the fire, it could not be controlled, even after the mine was flooded. Scars from this fire are still visible, and the mine was never reopened. Mining began tapering off due to economic conditions. Still, in 1905, records show that the Colorado Midland Railroad hauled 250 cars filled with coal from the New Castle mines.

During the peak of mining activity in the 1890s, New Castle was home to a population ranging from 1,500 to 2,500. Coal was transported by railway as fuel for the silver smelters in Aspen and Leadville. New Castle businesses included a cannery, a brickyard, a brewery, banks, a cement factory, dance halls, a printing office, saloons, restaurants, three livery stables, two bakeries and several hotels. The town became a small transportation hub with two train depots for the Denver & Rio Grande Western and the Colorado Midland.

In 1912, the Vulcan Mine was purchased by a new operator, Rocky Mountain Fuel Co., which started a new tunnel near the original tunnel that still smoldered from the fire that occurred 16 years before. There were rumors among the workers that mine gas was still a problem, but management did nothing to address the issue. On Dec. 18, 1913, residents of New Castle heard "a giant clap of thunder" as the

Vulcan exploded a second time.

Rescue was stymied by a massive cave-in, and it was a full day before the rubble was cleared to access the tunnel. All 37 miners in the tunnel were killed, and a long mourning period followed in New Castle. The president of the company arrived the day after the blast and offered surviving families $75 for each victim of the accident to help cover funeral expenses. A subsequent investigation by the state coal mine inspector found fault with Rocky Mountain Fuel, but concluded that $75 was "adequate" compensation for the bereaved.

A memorial in New Castle's Burning Mountain Park is dedicated to scores of coal miners who lost their lives in mine explosions in the late 19th and early 20th centuries at the nearby Vulcan Mine. MARK HILTON/HISTORICAL MARKER DATABASE

Four years after the deadly blast, the Vulcan exacted another human toll: Five men were killed in 1917 while clearing rubble from a cave-in. Shortly after the wagon bearing its grim cargo from Roderick's Ridge reached New Castle, a violent explosion from the Vulcan shook the earth, and yet another fire spread along the coal seam, which is still burning today inside what is known as Burning Mountain.

The local economy turned to ranching, agriculture, sawmills and fruit farming. According to the 1900 census, after mining dwindled, the population dropped to 431. For the next seven decades, the population slowly grew to about 600 to 800 residents. In the late 1980s, former ranchland north of downtown was built up into housing developments.

New Castle history remains palpable with signs marking the town's historic landmarks on 11 downtown buildings designated by the New Castle Historic Preservation Commission. A lifesize memorial statue honoring miners lost in a decades-long legacy of tragedy was dedicated in 2004 in Burning Mountain Park on Main Street.

BETTER JOBS, CLOSER TO HOME

ON THE 7-MILE DRIVE from New Castle to Silt, Gresley described how regionalism is creating a powerful synergy for economic development in the region. "The four municipal managers of New Castle, Silt, Rifle and Parachute/Battlement Mesa came together and said, 'We need a more regional approach,'" she said. "So, they collaborated about two years ago to see how we can move the needle on the mission—better jobs, closer to home. Because, when you have people in your community spending in your community, involved in your community, the community can thrive. How do we make realistic steps toward that?"

The first step, Gresley said, is to make local residents aware of job opportunities closer to home that could alleviate long upvalley commutes. Changes will come slowly as workers are reluctant to alter habitual patterns or give up wages and benefits.

"We're comfortable with what we've always known," Gresley said, "even if that is an hour-and-a-half drive each way. I did it, and it became part of my daily life because I had a career and a good salary and great benefits, and I had worked really hard to get that. And there are people who feel quite happy to have an escape by getting on the bus or having that quiet time in their cars. Not everyone is unhappy commuting, but it's about having the options. There are a lot of businesses here that don't have the ability to provide certain benefits that bigger companies can do. And that's something the Economic Development Partnership could do—become a marketplace for insurance benefits and other services."

Population growth within Colorado River Valley communities has been boosted by the pandemic and regional economics. Between 2010 and 2020, the combined populations of New Castle, Silt, Rifle, Parachute and Battlement Mesa increased 16%, according to census data, while growth remained stagnant in the Roaring Fork Valley (1.4%) despite a growing economy. Housing costs have been increasing regionally, with the median sale price in 2023 reaching $1.9 million in Carbondale and $919,500 in Glenwood Springs, while the Colorado River Valley remains relatively more attainable ($645,000 for a 2023 median sale price in New Castle and $467,000 in Rifle), according to reports published by the Aspen Board of Realtors.

"We are growing whether we like it or not," Gresley said, "because the cost of living is pushing people down here.

"Our local town governments are conservative and very wary of making sure we make the right decisions about growth. We are slow moving and not looking for growth for the sake of growth or to grow to support an industry that isn't necessarily benefiting our communities," Gresley said. "On the other end, if you don't grow, you don't adapt to conditions. You change or die. I hope to be the connector for that vision to show people the opportunities."

That's a tall order for a region that appears to be ripe for development. Yet, as Gresley and other town leaders emphasize, the quality of rural life has become a sacred covenant. Many residents have witnessed growth that has displaced locals, and they don't want to repeat that here.

"People here basically want a roof over their heads, food on the table, and enough left over to do something they enjoy or spend time with their kids or get their kids into college," Gresley said. "We don't need to have all the bells and whistles. It's a bit more of a simple outlook on life. That's what makes these communities a little different than Vail and Aspen. No one here really wants to grow to be at that level. We want to keep the identities of our individual towns. We're taking a regional approach, but every town has its uniqueness."

Men with a wagon full of luggage in front of the Rifle House on Railroad Avenue in Rifle about 1900. Most likely they were headed to the train station two blocks away. Offices of the Rifle Telegram newspaper can be seen in the background.
RIFLE HERITAGE CENTER

SILT IS MORE THAN FINE SAND

IN 1881, not long after the Utes had been ordered out of Colorado by Gov. Frederick Pitkin, John Harvey filed a claim on land nestled against the Grand Hogback, a prominent topographical feature of connected hills that form a straight line from Meeker to McClure Pass. Hog Back Pass became Harvey Gap, where a coal mine was later developed. This region was also known as "Old Squaw's Camp" for an elderly Ute woman who presided over a gathering place for Utes where horses were kept, plus a herd of 50 to 75 cattle.

The Denver & Rio Grande Western Railroad laid tracks along the Colorado River from Glenwood Springs to Silt in 1889. Soon, one- and two-story buildings lined the main street for six blocks, from the railroad depot to Cozza Gulch. In Silt's early days, there were pool halls, clothing stores, a theater and a dance hall.

Jeff Layman was Silt town administrator at the time he was interviewed for this story. He recently retired and is currently employed by the town to address selected projects.
CONTRIBUTED PHOTO

Silt became a farming and ranching community that incorporated in 1915, seven years after the Silt Bridge was built across the Colorado River to accommodate the homesteaders who lived up Divide Creek to the south.

Today, Silt has a population of 3,600, according to Jeff Layman, Silt's town administrator at the time of this interview in spring 2024.

"We don't have a lot of employment opportunities in Silt yet, so 90% to 95% of Silt residents go somewhere else to work, mostly tradesmen and hospitality workers who commute. They are willing to put up with that because of the paycheck. That drive is part of the bargain. I commute just three blocks to my office, and I feel for those people who have to make that drive and don't like it."

Born in Kansas, Layman moved to Silt in 2018 after spending 37 years in the Eagle Valley, where he worked 30 years in law enforcement. He served as police chief in Avon for seven years and as Eagle

County undersheriff for five. With a master's degree in public administration, Layman was hired as Silt's town administrator, where he found a perfect fit.

"Silt is affordable, and it's got a really nice small town vibe," said Layman, pointing out that Silt is the smallest town of the three along the Colorado River Valley. (According to Aspen Board of Realtors reports, the median sale price for a single-family home in Silt reached $540,000 in 2023.) "Silt attracts people who want a two-block main street, don't need all the bells and whistles, and who don't mind stopping at City Market on their way home because there's no grocery store here. Silt is for people who like a little more relaxed pace of life and a place where you can walk downtown and see your neighbors, stand around in the middle of Main Street and hobnob, listen to music, watch fireworks, and have your kids sit on Santa's lap. It feels like western Colorado."

Layman allowed that the river communities have moved away from "a history of parochialism" thanks to a new generation of municipal managers who have cemented collaborative relationships. "Over the last five years," said Layman, "we have made a real effort to compare notes, get in touch, and encourage our boards to meet their counterparts and talk about regional issues."

For example, Layman noted a collaborative rapport between Silt and the city of Glenwood Springs, which is crucial since Silt depends on the Colorado River as its municipal water source. During fires, mudslides and floods, Silt relies on good relations upstream with Glenwood Springs to protect its water quality.

"Our challenges are like everywhere else," said Layman, adding that housing is a key issue. The town has 96 apartment units under construction, with 70 more units of single-family housing and 104 more units on the drawing board. The town has an opportunity to build an events center on the Colorado River.

"We have a lot of great opportunities going," said Layman, "and we'd like to offer regional employment that will allow people to work in a meaningful job closer to home where they don't have to make that commute. That's our big challenge. But housing in Silt is getting more expensive now, so our board is working on addressing affordable

This handpicked production team of 22 at DM Vans staffs their expansive facility.
PAUL ANDERSEN/ASPEN JOURNALISM

housing before it becomes as acute as it is in the Roaring Fork Valley."

Layman's 37 years of experience in the Eagle Valley made him well suited to his administrative role in Silt. "I've seen growth, and I've lived it," said Layman, "so it's pretty easy for me to see the same kinds of challenges that are starting to show up in the Colorado River Valley. I've really become attached here to a place and a people who have made an impact on my life. I love the people I work with, and it's just a wonderful place."

DAVE AND MATT'S BIG MANUFACTURING ADVENTURE

ON THE 7-MILE DRIVE from Silt to Rifle, now the largest municipality in Garfield County, Gresley steered us to a small industrial park where a manufacturing dynamo is changing the complexion of the region. A vast parking lot is filled, bumper to bumper, with 80-plus camper vans, a fleet of Dodge Ram ProMasters being outfitted with state-of-the-art camper technology.

"It started off with two guys building vans—Dave and Matt, friends from college," said Arran Shrosbree, head of manufacturing for Dave and Matt Vans, or DM Vans, as the logo has it. "They came to vans from looking for an affordable place to live and a great way to access

COMMUNITY BLOSSOMS ALONG THE COLORADO RIVER · 85

the outdoors. The timing was fortuitous with the pandemic, when the van life just took off."

The company started in Gypsum in 2019 and, because rural Garfield County is more affordable, moved the manufacturing branch to Rifle in 2022, followed by the administrative side in 2023.

"We looked countrywide and settled on staying in Colorado," said Shrosbree, a transplanted Brit with a high-tech background, "because a lot of our team is from here, we're local, and we appreciate everything that Colorado offers and wanted to stay very grounded to that. We are all avid skiers, bikers, climbers and hikers."

DM Vans began with custom build-outs on whatever vans customers brought in. "We then partnered with local dealerships," said Shrosbree, "like Berthoud in Glenwood to get our hands on the chassis and control the whole build."

Arran Shrosbree, head of manufacturing for Dave and Matt Vans (DM Vans) displays one of over 50 "lifestyle vans" at their state-of-the-art production and manufacturing center near Rifle. PAUL ANDERSEN/ ASPEN JOURNALISM

In 2023, the highly skilled and selected 22 employees at DM Vans built 157 units with state-of-the-art cabinetry via computer cutting and milling, and expert finishing and assembly. The company sold about 130 units last year and earned $14 million. There are 511 DM vans on the road today, marketed as an alternative to buying a home and offering rugged mobility with total comfort.

"Our take on the RV space is that we are creating a tool for people to improve their lives," said Shrosbree. "The vans are perfect for travel nurses, yoga wellness teachers, ski instructors and those who choose vans as affordable housing. We want our product to be as reliable, efficient and as intentional as possible. We call our vans 'LVs,' or lifestyle vehicles, because we believe they are tools to improve your lifestyle."

"We're creating a Swiss Army knife of a vehicle," said Joe Smith, DM Vans' youthful president, who came to DM Vans with a wealth of retail and managerial experience, "because our vans have innumerable uses and are significantly less expensive than a house. We're young, and we have an extremely powerful team because we hire on values-fits. You have to find the right people and know what you're looking for. Making the leap to Rifle is our next iteration of business."

"We all share core values," said Shrosbree. "We're all driven to achieve excellence. We're all transparent with each other. We work together intentionally, not playing any games. We're all just looking to get to the best answer, and that makes for a pretty harmonious workspace. It's not all sunshine and rainbows, and I'm not painting it as a utopia, because we don't want to rule out friction. In challenging each other is where you find the genius."

DM vans are now sold nationwide, not only direct to consumers, but through dealership partners on both coasts. The company is planning to release custom Ford Transit vans beginning in 2026, and that design process is where the team's melting pot of ideas comes together, said Shrosbree.

The DM Vans workforce lives in New Castle, Rifle, Grand Junction and elsewhere. As testament to the van life, 14 of the 22 employees live full time in their vans either on-site, on nearby Bureau of Land Management property and, on weekends, in Moab and beyond. Equipped with solar panels and super-efficient, gas-powered heating, DM vans define a new level of off-grid mobile living.

"I have lived in my van for one year," said Smith, "and it works for me because I like to live somewhat simply. And rents are insane because, basically, you're paying for someone else's mortgage. Moving to Rifle, we have created our own small community, and as we plant our roots, we want to expand that. We're getting to know other businesses and more people here, and we're passionate about community."

Driving a short distance farther west on rural Highway 6, Gresley listed a handful of other business ventures that are taking root here: EcoDwelling is an ecologically attuned modular home manufacturer. Natural Soda is one of the largest producers of sodium bicarbonate in North America. "What I love about this," said Gresley, "is that it's about the past, present and future coming together and driving us forward as a sustainable community."

In Rifle, over lunch at the Whistle Pig, an eatery on the town's attractive Western-themed Main Street, Gresley introduced me to Mayor Sean Strode.

SIGHTING IN ON RIFLE

RIFLE IS LAID OUT on a grid of streets in a valley surrounded by mesas and mountains. Rifle, the largest municipality in Garfield County, with a population of 10,600, is 40% Latino, making it the region's most ethnically diverse community. According to Strode (Strod-ee), the city is energized by an emerging entrepreneurial spirit born, in large part, out of its Latino culture.

Strode represents a new generation of leadership in this historical farming and ranching community, founded in 1882 and incorporated in 1905. President Teddy Roosevelt came hunting here in 1901, lending a sportsman's character to the region.

There are three theories from the 1880s regarding the town's unique name, two of which relate tales of absent-minded pioneers leaving their rifles leaning against trees. Another legend claims that the town was named for the frontier custom of firing one's rifle to signal an approach.

In 1882, Abram W. Maxfield was the first man to travel west of Glenwood Springs with a wagon, having to take it apart to pack it around cliffs and ledges and then put it back together. He was the first known Anglo settler in Rifle. Farming and ranching were the original industries in the area, and Rifle became a trade center when the railroad came through in 1899.

Sean Strode is the mayor Rifle, serving his second term. PAUL ANDERSEN/ASPEN JOURNALISM

Rifle's economy fluctuated with dependence on historic coal mining. The most recent resource development took place in the early 1980s with the promise of massive oil shale extraction that was to convert western Garfield County into a global energy producer. Workers had come from all over the world to profit from oil shale, and Rifle's population doubled with a nearly overnight boom, jumping to about 4,500 from 2,700.

Rifle went bust on Black Sunday, May 2, 1982, the day Exxon,

88 · IN SEARCH OF COMMUNITY

the Colony oil shale developer, quit the project, locked the gates, and left more than 2,000 people suddenly unemployed. Workers fled in droves. It was said that the only local business still viable was U-Haul rentals. The economic collapse was felt countywide.

Despite the devastating impacts of the 1982 crash, Colorado River communities had benefited during the buildup as oil companies invested millions of dollars in infrastructure improvements. The region began rebounding financially after a 3/4-cent sales tax passed in 1996. Today, local governments along the Colorado River are wary of monolithic enterprises that could wreak similar boom-bust havoc, a traditional liability of the extractive industries.

Rifle's culture fosters a growing arts community, with performances at the renovated historic Ute Theater and with decorative murals and other visual arts. A historic modern art sensation focused the world's attention on Rifle from 1970 to 1972, when big-wrap artist Christo and his wife, Jeanne-Claude, chose the canyon that Rifle Creek carved in the Grand Hogback as the site of a unique and elaborate display known as Christo's Valley Curtain.

Christo's curtain fabric was a parachute-like material of 250,000 square feet that weighed 6 tons. It rose above the valley floor suspended 350 feet at the ends on steel cables. The sagging center had an archway at the bottom to permit traffic on Highway 325. Anchors weighed 70 tons, and the fabric was fastened by 59 stressed steel rods that went 40 feet into the sandstone canyon walls.

Construction started in 1970 at a cost of $250,000 with teams of engineers, site supervisors, 35 construction workers and 64 temporary staff made up of college students and itinerant art workers. The first attempt to raise the curtain failed as wind blew it down. The second attempt, in August 1972, was successful, until wind blew it down the next day. The final cost was more than $600,000, and the only evidence is photographic.

Rifle's economy today is diversified with agriculture, oil and gas, and tourism. Rifle Falls State Park is a popular destination 14 miles north of Rifle. The falls spill over a limestone cliff where, in 1910, the town of Rifle built the Rifle Hydroelectric Plant. Rifle has gained an international reputation, drawing world-class climbers to crags at

Christo's Valley Curtain put Rifle on the map in 1970-1972 through an unlikely identification with modern art. NATIONAL GALLERY OF ART

Rifle Mountain Park, touted as the best limestone sport climbing in North America. Mountain biking has also taken off, thanks to the Rifle Area Mountain Bike Organization (RAMBO), which was started in 2012 as a trail-advocacy program that now boasts many miles of single track for all levels and ages with trailhead parking a few miles north of town along the Grand Hogback. In the valley, more than 20 miles of bike and pedestrian trails crisscross the city.

Strode, founding director of RAMBO, moved here in 2012 with a musical background that includes a bachelor's degree from the Berklee College of Music in Boston, where he studied guitar, and a master's degree in jazz from Northwestern University. Originally from Wisconsin, Strode was a member of the music faculty at the University of Texas, San Antonio, and at University of Colorado Boulder, where he met his future wife.

"My wife is from Rifle," said Strode, "so we came up to visit, and I fell in love. We moved here and never looked back. When I got here, I started learning about community—that you can volunteer time and become part of something. I realized you can make a difference in a small town."

Strode first volunteered on the Rifle Planning and Zoning Commission for four years, then was elected to Town Council, where he served for six years. He was elected mayor in 2021 and reelected to a second term in November 2023. Multiple roles have given Strode an intimate understanding of Rifle.

"For a long time, Rifle was a gas and oil bedroom community," he said. "Now, friends say, 'I own a house here, but I live in Aspen,' because they drive up there and spend all their time there. Progressively, this has become more and more of a community by creating a sense of place through events like town holidays. We are making downtown a place where people want to be."

Strode said the Rifle economy is based on "hardworking people" who display a drive for entrepreneurship, such as opening a restaurant, a painting business or a construction company. The median age is 31, and 51% of the population is female. "People here want to pursue their own passion and independence," said Strode. "The trades are very big here, and we have a very successful hospital, movie theaters, a vibrant airport and county administrative buildings. All of it is making us less dependent on other economies."

The Ute Theater host varied entertainments.
PAUL ANDERSEN/ASPEN JOURNALISM

Still, Strode advocates for regionalism by joining with economic partners to coordinate on challenges from Aspen to Parachute. "The issues we're encountering are not per town. They are per region," said Strode, "There is strength in teamwork, so I work hand in hand with the mayor of Glenwood and the mayor of Carbondale. We take a lot of pride in our town, but what we're doing is looking at the bigger picture."

Patrick Waller, Rifle's director of planning, said, "We've always been connected regionally because of jobs. We get more and more folks coming here and chatting about economic opportunities. Folks who need larger facilities find it very expensive upvalley, and any-

Rifle Park is a community gathering place for kids and families.
PAUL ANDERSEN/ASPEN JOURNALISM

thing that can locate a business here is a benefit to our region. Rifle is very careful about growth because the oil-and-gas bust still resonates here. It devastated the local economy."

Major employers in Rifle today are the hospital, Walmart and Colorado Mountain College. A regional airport boosts Rifle's connectivity far beyond its boundaries and often serves Aspen's private jets.

The Civic Plaza in Rifle is a community focal point that attests to Rifle's investment in its promising future.

Top among growth concerns, said Strode, is affordable, attainable housing. "That's an issue everywhere. We're partnering with Habitat for Humanity for income-based housing units expected to start this year."

"We are growing," said Strode, "and I want to be conscious of that and grow smartly, intelligently—honoring our history while moving forward. We are working with Garfield Clean Energy, and we're energy net-zero, or close to it, with solar on all of our government facilities." Strode added that making fiber internet available to people who own and run businesses is a pressing goal for the future.

Waller said Rifle's planning department identifies tiers of de-

Wapiti Commons is a Habitat for Humanity housing project in Rifle. Habitat is also working on building a production/construction warehouse on land owned by the city of Rifle. The warehouse will be leased at a nominal amount for 50-plus years to bring jobs, training and the construction of Habitat homes to the Western Slope. PAUL ANDERSEN/ASPEN JOURNALISM

velopment in areas already connected with water and sanitation, ideally within city boundaries served by adequate roads. "We want to avoid sprawl, which doesn't make sense fiscally," Waller said. "Rifle is set up well for the future. We have water rights annexed in from new development, and our current Tier 1 sites can accommodate 5,000 new residents, for a population of 15,000. Houses here are reaching $500,000, which you would not have thought of even five or six years ago."

Politically, Strode celebrates community diversity. "Rifle is a great city," he said. "We have strong, differing views on council, but we're all able to come together, amicably, state our positions, democratically take a vote, and move on. There is no animosity, and I think that's representative of our community. I'm constantly impressed."

Waller, who grew up in Glenwood Springs, brings to his role community-planning experience in Pitkin and Garfield counties. "Rifle is a cohesive community," he said, "with people who serve on committees and work together. We certainly have economic disparity here, but it's not billionaires versus affordable-housing folks. Second homes are not an issue; we don't have that here, and there are only eight listings for Airbnb. You go by the pool in summer and it's exploding with kids. Rifle reminds me of a small town because it doesn't have the tourism these other towns have. Walking around town, folks flag me down and talk. And it's really cool in that way."

"Community is what supports you," said Strode. "Community is what makes your life good, whether it's people building trails or businesses supporting one another. Community is about support, camaraderie and acceptance. It is why we live where we live. As the largest municipality in Garfield County, we think a rising tide lifts all boats, and that's good for Rifle and our neighbors. If there is something we can do to help support Silt or Parachute or wherever, that makes our region better and makes Rifle better."

CHAPTER 8

Building Livable Communities

*Community Builders teaches
the value of cohesion*

A roundtable including stakeholders in the Colorado River Valley Economic Development Partnership works to identify future community challenges, during a Building Better Places training in the spring 2024 facilitated by the Glenwood Springs-based nonprofit Community Builders.
RYAN MACKLEY/ALIGN MULTIMEDIA

THE MASSIVE GRAND AVENUE BRIDGE that sweeps over the Colorado River in Glenwood Springs represents an ironic response to the affordable housing crisis facing the Roaring Fork Valley.

"That bridge is a $125 million dollar affordable housing project," Clark Anderson, founder and CEO of Community Builders, a Glenwood Springs-based nonprofit, said of the bridge that replaced a more-constrained crossing in 2017. "We weren't willing to invest in creating affordable housing close to where people work, so we reshaped Glenwood Springs to ship people up and down the valley all day. We say we don't have any money for affordable housing, but when you look at it that way, it's not for lack of resources. It's that we really don't want to see things change that are going to change anyway."

Anderson and his team advocate for healthy, equitable, resilient and sustainable communities through studied interventions and carefully tailored trainings. The team attracted national media attention in 2023 when the *New York Times* described how Community Builders helped to broker a community rift in Silverton, Colorado, where bitter political contention had resulted in death threats to the town's mayor.

The Silverton kerfuffle was instigated when the mayor refused to allow the recitation of the Pledge of Allegiance at Town Council meetings, a final straw that broke the community's already frayed equilibrium. Only through diplomatic reaffirmation of community cohesion did Silverton mend the bitter antipathies and protracted contention that were inciting potential violence.

Community Builders and, specifically, Anderson were acknowledged as the healing balm that brought combative citizens together through orchestrated civil dialogue. Anderson, who led the effort, was already working in Silverton to help draft a 10-year master plan for the town, so the timing was right for an intervention.

The Grand Avenue Bridge in Glenwood Springs spans the Colorado River. It was completed in 2017 at a cost of $125 million. ASPEN DAILY NEWS

In the heat of the controversy, Anderson convened small groups in what became known as The Compass Project. "Community Builders would bring residents together, away from microphones and public spaces, to see if they could find a common vision for Silverton's future," the *Times* reported.

And so they did, resulting in a strategy that established a shared sense of place by acknowledging among its citizens a common love for Silverton. Anderson and team first had to build the trust required to foment this all-important sense of mutuality. They did so through open dialogue, often among embittered foes.

"It turned out that newcomers and old-timers, millennials and baby boomers pretty much wanted the same thing for Silverton," reported the *Times*. A focus on shared values ameliorated hostile perceptions as the town took the first step in community healing.

Anderson has also brokered community divisions in Crested Butte, where growth was the issue, and in Taos, New Mexico, where the community was fractured by racially driven social divisions.

"We look for projects in communities that can demonstrate need," Anderson said. "We bring ideas, information and expertise. But rather than being a hired external expert, we understand that the fundamental knowledge you need is in the community where there is an understanding of needs and values. We're not hired to find the answers. We come in and say, 'We will help you find the answers,' and in that process, you help build community. By virtue of taking ownership and responsibility, there is a stronger feeling of purpose."

THE EVOLUTION OF COMMUNITY

WHY DOES COMMUNITY MATTER? Why does loss of community cause deep lament for those who have lived and loved it—as evidenced by the discourse around the loss of soul that surfaces regularly in Aspen today?

"At the most basic level, community is relationships," Anderson said. "As an ecologist, part of my thinking comes from science and nature. We humans evolved to benefit from social interaction and cooperation in which we evolved certain behaviors and characteristics that made it easier for us to bond and have cohesion, which is something that's very deeply ingrained in our being because it is part of how we're hardwired.

"Unfortunately, we also inherited very real dispositions toward competition amongst each other for resources, which turns into tribalism. And we know that these are aspects that come from the primate lineage. Our closer primate lineage is more aligned for competition and tribalism, and there's another lineage that's more oriented toward caregiving. It's all part of us."

Anderson said primate influences are conflicted by the same dualism that separates humans from much of the animal kingdom. "We can be animals that want to belong, that want to be connected and that fundamentally need to be part of something larger than ourselves to survive," he said. "We can inherently be interested in our own needs and self-interest. But we can also struggle to see shared values in people who are different than us. That's part of what we have to deal with in the human mindset."

This incongruity between self and others can divide communities and muddy the value of communal relations upon which societies are built. "When you look at what we've done as a species, the most magical thing is that we have come together in certain places to create cultural and physical reflections of who we are, not as individuals but as a group with shared ideas, principles and values," he said.

Communities, he said, are a physical manifestation of times and places where "people come and settle together and together reflect a physical and economic manifestation of a place. Progress, innovation and technology took place in the cities thousands of years ago where people were there to exchange ideas, information and technology. Communities are our highest form of manifesting what's best about us: art, music, culture, architecture and belonging."

Clark Anderson, founder and CEO of the Glenwood Springs-based non-profit Community Builders. RYAN MACKLEY/ALIGN MULTIMEDIA

Collective aspirations, said Anderson, "are the most important things we humans have created—and not all of those are pretty. There are times in history when some of those shared values are quite ugly, but there's a lot of beauty, too."

Most historic changes have occurred slowly in what Anderson calls "incrementalism," which allows social traits to establish gradually, in ways that work empirically. As technology and capitalism increased the speed of change, such as the suburban model that put masses of people into clustered homes, the rate of change thwarted assimilation to new lifestyles and emergent values.

"It was very different from what had been," Anderson said of suburbia. "People became separated by economic status, and that became written in code—bigger and smaller houses, expensive and less expensive. So, communities began to look different. There are now a lot more pressures on community, and people are scared by what's happening to their communities. That has to do with the isolation that comes from our economic widening gap and the isolation we get from technology."

The struggle for community is confounded by dissociation from those around us. "Community," in Anderson's definition, "is when we're connected and are the best versions of ourselves, which means looking out for each other and doing things that are altruistic. Reciprocation is an amazingly powerful thing."

MOTIVATED BY CHANGE

ANDERSON, 47, grew up in East Vail when "Vail was still a town." His parents met in Vail, where his father, a Vietnam War veteran, was advised to seek peace for himself. "My father died at 42, in 1984. At the time, he was serving on the Vail Town Council. I was 7, and that had a huge effect on my life. What I learned later is that the things he was working for on council were the things I would later adopt as my own interests today: housing, water, and how you sustain community and quality of life while going through change."

A strong ethic in land conservation inspired studies in ecology at the University of Colorado Boulder, where Anderson met a man who would become his mentor. Will Toor, a former mayor of Boulder, today serves as executive director of the Colorado Energy Office, which is an arm of the state government.

"Toor was on City Council in Boulder," Anderson said, "and he talked about this idea of infill. I told him that sounded like development, but he said, 'No, we need to figure out how not to sprawl.'" Toor introduced Anderson to community planning at a new level and set him on a career path that would lead him to found Community Builders years later.

By the 1990s, Anderson had returned to Eagle/Vail, where he aligned with childhood friend Peter Hart, who later became a wilderness advocate attorney with Wilderness Workshop in the Roaring Fork Valley. Another associate, Arn Menconi, was then an Eagle County commissioner. A fourth team member, Adam Palmer, died in an avalanche near Silverton in 2021.

These friends started a community leadership forum—"Shaping the Future of the Eagle Valley"—in which Anderson played a role coordinating a group of 25 leaders in the Eagle Valley asking: How do we grow and handle transportation and the economy?

"This was in the '90s," said Anderson, "and a lot of those questions were not fully formed, and there were various futures that the Vail Valley could have taken. It was an intriguing conversation. We applied what we learned to the Eagle County Comprehensive Plan update."

Research led Anderson to help form comprehensive plans for

other communities, including Basalt and Aspen, which added "smart growth" to his vernacular. This is defined as mixed land uses; compact building design; a range of housing opportunities and choices; walkable neighborhoods; distinctive, attractive communities with a strong sense of place; and the preservation of open space, farmland, natural beauty and critical environmental areas. This led him to graduate school at the University of California, Davis, where his wife was earning a doctorate in ecology.

"I spent a lot of time studying community engagement and decision-making and how to enable effective collaboration at the local level—to understand and decide around difficult issues," Anderson said.

Community Builders staff members Joe Babeu and Mackinzi Taylor draw ideas from a team from West End Montrose County.
RYAN MACKLEY/ALIGN MULTIMEDIA

He was hired by the Sonoran Institute, which pioneered what would become smart growth principles. By running its water program with a conservationist goal, Anderson realized that, in the conservation world, the big missing puzzle piece was community planning.

"Conservation had been a defense, where you lock up land and water," Anderson said. "But we needed an offense, which is to carry the ball of growth and change. We can't just sit back and say, 'I'm good,' and watch from our comfortable places as the rest of the world suffers. Growth and change are not only happening now; they will always happen. As an ecologist at heart, I understand that as a fact of life."

Resistance to change often stands in the way of forming a practical collective vision for the future. The challenge of acknowledging change as it occurs induces struggles within communities.

"We're trying to work toward a static idea that's often in the rearview," said Anderson. "That doesn't mean we shouldn't say no to things or be clear about our priorities and principles, but it does mean that we're too often fighting the wrong battles. That means we're making a lot less progress on the things that matter because a lot of the dialogue happens in this nonreality that's absent change."

Anderson said that building roadblocks to change merely displaces change elsewhere. His example of the Grand Avenue Bridge in Glenwood Springs speaks to pushing change farther downvalley and creating impacts there.

"The Roaring Fork Valley has had a massive effect on shaping the Colorado River Valley," Anderson said. "That happens when we don't understand the consequence of our decisions because we don't deal with the real facts on the ground."

VISIONARY COMMUNITY PLANNING

ANDERSON OPENED the Colorado office of the Sonoran Institute and found that his community planning background fit with Sonoran's model for conservation. He came to realize the mistake of separating a conservation ethic from community planning.

"I wasn't working in Aspen or Vail," said Anderson. "I was working in Rifle and Delta because that's where the pressures were and a lot of the need was. But you come into the room there as a conservation guy, and you don't get any respect."

Anderson recognized the limitations of saying no to growth, so he formed Community Builders in 2016 to provide the alternative of "a very positive, forward-looking community and economic development organization that allowed us to take on a broader suite of issues."

Community Builders has opened doors to communities in transition. "We worked to help communities going through transition away from coal to think about and develop economic strategies for how they are going to do that," he said. "It's called 'just transition work.' Not everything had to come back to: Did we protect the land and the water? Other outcomes were equally important."

With a staff of nine, Community Builders has drawn funding from earned income, as well as grants from the Economic Development Administration in Washington, D.C., underwriting projects in energy-driven northwestern Colorado and with Native American communities in Arizona and southwest Colorado. Anderson also raises philanthropic funds to seed new initiatives and cover the cost of projects such as Silverton, where Community Builders was the largest investor and which made the project feasible.

A community intervention begins with basic questions, said Anderson: "What is it you really want to see in the future here? What is your hope for your town? What are you afraid of? In the responses, you begin to find information that can help the community by building a better understanding of what isn't working and what the possibilities are. And once you've got that, you start to get a vision. From that vision, we can bring in some expertise, like examples of what other communities are doing, and create a learning environment where community members come in and talk with us about what has worked in other places and how they've navigated some of the trade-offs. We help them build toward crafting solutions that are going to work there.

Jamie LaRue of Garfield County Libraries, left, and Evan Zislis of the Aspen Institute's Hurst Initiative explore ideas for sustainable communities.
RYAN MACKLEY/ALIGN MULTIMEDIA

"That takes a hell of a lot of time building trust and getting through tough discussions, but by the time you go through that, people are pretty bought in. They believe in the work because they've had a chance to talk and had a chance to drive some of it. They're helping guide the ship."

WOEBEGONE TIMES

LAMENTS FOR THE IRRETRIEVABLE PAST are compelling, said Anderson, who understands place-based emotions from the pangs of loss he felt for the Vail of his childhood.

"There are good things that can come in its place, with challenges and opportunities," he said. "Most mountain towns have faced essentially the same set of dynamics. They are such intriguing places to live that they attract a lot of people, and they have service economies. As it gets harder and harder for people to make it, the core of the community can't be there anymore. The choice is often preference for physical characteristics over the characters that make up our communities.

"I like to think of community character as two things: the physical look and feel of a place and the more fundamental thing, the characters that give that place its character. Some of these towns have tried to create a place that has character, but when you take the characters out, it just feels plastic. For us to be able to keep the characters, we are going to radically have to rethink what this place will look like in 30 years, but we're committed enough to the people and to the idea of community that we're going to design this to make it happen."

Anderson cited places that have preserved community character in Europe and Latin America, places that have great charm as small communities and have realistically figured out how to accommodate a lot of people. Anderson then zeros in on the Roaring Fork Valley with sobering clarity.

"So, growth is managed to look OK, and it's going to be really expensive, which means certain people can be here, but at least we won't change. We'll be OK," he said. "But the huge miss we made is that it's not going to stay the same. If we don't keep the characters, people are going to feel the same discontentment, and what's worse is that we will have accidentally shared this challenging set of problems with our neighbors in a very predictable domino-cascading effect.

"The characteristics of communities get hollowed out because a lot of people who once lived there can't afford to be there anymore. And it's important to remember that community isn't static and has to include an idea of the future."

That future belongs to succeeding generations, yet Anderson acknowledged that his two school-age children will probably not be able to afford to live here as adults.

"The idea of feeling rooted in a place changes when there doesn't seem to be a future for my kids and therefore there's not a future for me," he said. "We wring our hands wondering what happened to community, but we didn't make space for them. When I look at this valley, my dream would be that we can rethink who really is part of our community with a much more expansive look.

"We look beyond what we have today and ask: What if we took a

The Colorado River Valley Economic Development Partnership (CRVEDP) team with facilitator Clark Anderson. RYAN MACKLEY/ALIGN MULTIMEDIA

radical re-imagining of what this place would be like if we all worked together to create a valley or region that's connected with neighborhoods with real people living in them that feel like they're connected to this place, but also feel like they can move throughout this region that we're all part of, and we're not just cogs in a machine feeding a set of jobs that are supporting a pretty small part of the community?"

Bitterness over loss of community foments a lack of cohesion and civil dialogue, which tends to divide rather than unite, consigning the region to a lack of cooperation and a default to the pitfalls of isolation and economic disparity.

"Now, in Glenwood, we can't even approve an eight-unit Habitat for Humanity project on city land that is being made out to be a unique meadow when, in reality, it is surrounded by roads. It's one place where we can create homes for people who make this place work, and we can't even do that. I would love to see these places remain exactly as they are, but I also want my kids to be able to live here."

This is where Anderson the conservationist confronts Anderson the community builder.

"We are surrounded by the mountains," he said, "and I'm a conservationist who believes we have to stop pretending that every inch of land matters. Let's get serious about how we create real neighborhoods and do it in a systems-looking way that's not just a housing project connected by the same type of auto-oriented transportation system we have. Let's create a connective system of neighborhoods and locally serving jobs that makes this place whole. This is totally doable, but it takes political will. If we truly care about community, we need to radically rethink our fear of growth and embrace that we need to begin making space for our community.

"That community is here, and they deserve to be here just as much as we do, so let's figure out how to build a community economy that works. That will take a massive political mind shift. Until we do that, all this feeling of losing people, of being stuck in traffic, it's not going to go away."

A PRACTICAL, LOCAL APPLICATION

IN EARLY MARCH 2024, Anderson and his team at Community Builders facilitated a three-day symposium at the Hotel Colorado titled, "Building Better Places" that brought together representatives of five different governance organizations from across western Colorado to exchange ideas and share stories. Included were 10 civic and political leaders from towns collaborating under the umbrella of the Colorado River Valley Economic Development Partnership (CRVEDP), which covers New Castle, Silt, Rifle, Parachute and Battlement Mesa. Orchestrated by Community Builders, the symposium brought participants together to understand and address key challenges and opportunities facing their communities in order to find common ground on workable action plans.

Alicia Gresley, a Rifle City Council member who heads the CRVEDP, explained that her search for economic development consultation a year ago led to Anderson and Community Builders, which tailors programs and helps fund them. Gresley applied, and the CRVEDP was accepted for the Building Better Places workshop, the tenets of which dovetailed with the partnership's ambition to generate a sustainable regional economy with the tagline "better jobs closer to home." The symposium also included groups from Meeker, Montrose County, Silverton, Leadville, and Lake County.

"Progress is hard," Anderson states on the Community Builders website. "Breaking from the status quo relies on undoing decades of outdated and inequitable systems, policies and paradigms that guide the decisions and investments that shape our communities and economies."

Timing is crucial, he emphasized, and now is the right time to inspire the Colorado River communities as they grapple to form a common vision from shared values that can move them forward.

"Once you have people willing to make the move, you're ready," said Anderson, who likened the process to an individual who wakes one day with the desire for more clarity in doing things in alignment with one's values by examining routines and habits that one is willing to work on.

"We start with key trends, things like housing, a changing economy, political divisions," Anderson said. "Then we move into planning and policy, building capacity and creating funding, engagement and support. We provide success stories they can learn from."

The three-day March program convened a mix of private and public civic leaders who formed, stormed and normed in the interests of their individual communities, but with the goal of adopting regional unity.

"It was so great to get to know members of our organization in a different way and with new perspectives," Gresley said. "It was a great learning environment as a listening and sounding board for our common ground, although we have different approaches."

A large and growing client list has provided Community Builders with examples of communities across the West that are engaging in successful cooperation.

"We believe in the power of story," Anderson said. "Throughout our work, we've seen how stories can drive meaningful change. From success stories to lessons learned, we use these insights to engage and inspire audiences through public speaking, media production and traditional and digital media outreach. From small towns to growing cities, we assist in grounding strong local partnerships and engaging the entire community in an effort to create healthy, equitable and prosperous places."

Community Builders acknowledges that "too often, the decisions that impact an entire community are made by a handful of people.

This is poor civic health. We believe every member of a community is capable of understanding issues and giving an impactful voice. Effective civic engagement meets people where they are, empowering them to take part in their community."

Gresley has become a driving force for this outcome. "It was good to have an independent third party to facilitate and pull out our different points of view and lead us toward agreement on the fundamentals," she said. "The training revealed that the energy and commitment is there. We all left with the same intention, that when we all put in these efforts, it benefits the whole region."

Gresley pointed out that the outcomes of the symposium may one day influence the lives of thousands of citizens along the Colorado River, which has seen high population growth in the past two decades.

"There's a lot of opportunity for economic development here," said Gresley, "and we are taking the lessons from the Exxon pullout that wiped out Parachute in the 1980s not to put all our eggs in one basket but, rather, to diversify the region as a whole."

BLACK MONDAY AND THE OIL SHALE BUST

A SINGLE-FOCUS ECONOMY led to the economic disaster historically known as "Black Monday," when on May 2, 1982, energy giant Exxon, then the largest energy company in the world, announced that it was pulling out of its Colony oil shale project based in Parachute and Battlement Mesa. Exxon's notice came as a surprise to local and state government officials and instantly put more than 2,000 people out of work, plunging Garfield County and the surrounding region into a recession that had a lasting ripple effect on the economy of the entire state.

But nowhere was the impact as great as in western Garfield County, which had become overextended as a result of speculation based on the promise of an unprecedented energy boom.

"When Exxon pulled the plug, Western Slope counties were left with huge debts for police and fire protection and new hospitals," Andrew Gulliford, a professor at Fort Lewis College, wrote in High Country News in 2012. "I watched my friends lose their jobs, their houses and, finally, their marriages. The president of the First National Bank in Grand Junction shot himself. The First National Bank in Rifle closed because so many people demanded their money. Desperate depositors lined the block."

Gulliford, who in 1989 detailed the oil shale debacle in his book "Boomtown Blues: Colorado Oil Shale," first written as a doctoral dissertation, was deeply moved by the cataclysm that paralyzed the region and sent shock waves across the West that reverberate in the region today. He wrote: "I couldn't help but think of all the local lives shattered by Exxon's corporate hubris, the decade-long economic depression shared by Grand Junction and Rifle, the bankruptcies, the foreclosures, the blighted lives, the lost hopes."

Oil shale development in the 1980s, he wrote, "was about international energy markets and corporate machismo. But no longer will energy companies run roughshod over Western Slope residents. The demographics have changed. Newcomers now unite with farm and ranch families."

With a valuable, if painful, lesson from history, residents of what Gulliford calls "The Next West" today speak up for environmentally responsible management of the area's public lands: "Let's wait for a proven technology that does not squander water, pollute the air and threaten wildlife and archaeological sites," he wrote. "The Old West was boom and bust. The Next West must embody environmentally and socially responsible development."

The promise of "The Next West" is what Gresley, the CRVEDP and Community Builders are working toward with a new paradigm for healthy, sustainable, thriving and, ultimately, livable communities by fashioning a new economic culture for a region in transition.

This transition is spelled out in the town of Parachute's municipal policy with clarity and purpose: "The Town Council values the oil and gas industry that fuels the local economy and also welcomed the marijuana industry when it was an emerging market. The Town Council now endeavors to further diversify the local economy and strives to create a strong and resilient tax base that can provide reliable services to the community throughout and despite economic downturns.

"The Town Council also wishes to create opportunities that reduce the necessity for our friends and families to endure daily 'super commutes' out of the community to higher-paying jobs elsewhere. The Town Council recognizes that this will require a high degree of flexibility and the ability to 'think big,' but it is fully embracing this challenge."

In 2022, the Town Council issued this mission statement: "Make Parachute the best place to live, work and raise a family in western Colorado. This includes diversifying the local economy, beautifying the community and creating additional amenities for existing residents and businesses."

Gulliford foresaw such ambitions in the aftermath of the Exxon disaster: "Again," he wrote, "the Colorado River Valley is at the fulcrum of a national debate, but now the issues are environmental protection as well as energy development. Quality of life is important."

Between 2015 and 2022, the percentage of home sales considered affordable to those making the median wage shrunk from 23% to 9% in Pitkin County, and from 78% to 37% in Garfield County, according to research conducted by the West Mountain Regional Housing Coalition.
DANIEL BAYER/ASPEN JOURNALISM

CHAPTER 9

The Housing Conundrum

*Where social justice
confronts economics*

MASLOW'S *HIERARCHY OF NEEDS* lists shelter as a fundamental requirement for a secure life. But thousands of people living and working in our economic region—from Aspen to Parachute—are coping with housing insecurity.

"We need upward of 6,000 homes just to house the people adequately who are already here," said Gail Schwartz, director of Habitat for Humanity of the Roaring Fork Valley. "People who are traveling four hours a day; multiple families living in a two-bedroom apartment; people living in garages. Their instability because of cost and utilities is what is so disruptive to our economy and our communities.

"This is a social justice issue, when you have people traveling long distances and leaving children to fend for themselves. It is wrong for our region. Affordable housing is the underpinning of our success as a community, long term."

Schwartz, a former Colorado state senator, has been a leader in affordable housing in western Colorado for a half-century. Her vocation began more than 50 years ago when she worked for Snow Engineering, a community planning firm that focused on mountain resorts across North America.

With then-Aspen Mayor Stacy Standley, Schwartz worked to gain recognition for housing as a crucial issue for Aspen in the early 1970s, when the writing was already on the wall. "We created a metric for resorts that when you sell so many lift tickets, you need services and employees and housing," Schwartz recalled. "It was about finding what creates a balanced community."

Toward that end, Schwartz helped to initiate the formation of the Aspen/Pitkin County Housing Authority (APCHA), where, in four years, she said the agency brought 800 homes online, housing units that are foundational to the APCHA program, which today oversees about 3,200 units.

"I know we can do this," said Schwartz, who took the helm of the local chapter of the nonprofit Habitat for Humanity in 2020. "We work with families as partners and build homes. We started out one house at a time, building with volunteers. Now we're building whole neighborhoods. It is something I'm absolutely passionate about."

HOUSING AS A MORAL ISSUE

SCHWARTZ IS NOT ALONE on an issue that has gained traction as the foremost moral challenge facing the Roaring Fork Valley and beyond. April Long, program director at West Mountain Regional Housing Coalition, is equally passionate about housing the valley's workforce and community.

"Our community," Long said, "would be better off if we can alleviate the stress for those within it who want to own their home, which for most means living farther away and accepting the commute. Having to accept that level of stress in your life and the time away from your family or your own needs for mental and physical health is unfair. It is a moral obligation to take care of each other and those who are struggling to care for themselves."

Long recalled growing up in a rural Alabama community that was struck by a tornado when she was 15. "It tore down homes and churches," she said. "People died. That was a coming-of-age experience for me where I recognized the collective suffering of a community from loss."

Long differentiates "workforce housing" from "community housing." The former, she said, is "housing made available or accessible for those who are working in the community, while the latter is about housing the entire community, like family members who may not be part of the local or regional workforce. It wouldn't be the community it is without those people, like retirees. If I work here, but also need my mother to be nearby to either help with my children or for me to help with her, then she's part of this community, too. And that allows this community to be robust and to thrive."

Long pointed out that housing must include all social strata: "If you're thinking about your own employees, you also need to think about your employee's teacher and other members of the larger community that make this a livable and enjoyable place."

A valley resident since 2008, Long has lived in Aspen, Carbondale, Missouri Heights, Basalt and, currently, Glenwood Springs. She owned a home in Missouri Heights and sold it at what she thought was the best time, at the outbreak of COVID-19 in 2020. After renting in Basalt, she realized she was suddenly priced out of buying a home in that area again.

"That happened really quickly, and was such a shock. I felt very disappointed having lived here for 15 years. I was making a fine living, but I was priced out of my community that I felt very close to. Luckily, I was able to buy in Glenwood Springs where I love living, but I was still commuting up and back to Aspen in a constant pull. My work was upvalley, but my life was downvalley, and there was a large commute and a lot of time spent between those two places."

Regional commuting is not a hardship for all, as Long, a frequent passenger on Roaring Fork Transit Agency buses, explained: "When that worked for me, I was able to relax, read the paper, and get some work done on the bus. But if you're not able to use public transportation, it's pretty stressful to sit in traffic that long and know that there is a life waiting for you at home.

"With small kids, I couldn't get home fast enough to make dinner, run the bath, do the homework, get them to bed. You're constantly waiting for the cars to move. It's comparable to traffic in any of our big urban areas where commutes are horrific. You expect it less here, but you make some trade-offs because you want the quality of life that this place offers, and traffic jams are incongruent with what you're expecting.

"So, housing is important to me, something I'm passionate about, and it's also important to our entire community. Without addressing it, I'm afraid our community could begin to collapse. I want this to be a place where my three children are able to work and live. I see the complications and struggle that housing places on families, and I'm hoping that this coalition is one of the tools that helps ease that."

Gail Schwartz, the director of Habitat for Humanity for the Roaring Fork Valley, has been a leader in affordable housing in western Colorado for a half-century. At Habitat, "we started out one house at a time, building with volunteers. Now we're building whole neighborhoods. It is something I'm absolutely passionate about."
PAUL ANDERSEN/ASPEN JOURNALISM

A SOBERING PICTURE

MEETING THIS MORAL OBLIGATION requires overcoming multiple roadblocks, as the *Aspen Daily News* reported in a Jan. 25 story about a housing forum put on by the West Mountain Regional Housing Coalition in Willits. "Speakers . . . last week presented a sobering picture of housing availability in the Roaring Fork Valley," staff writer Austin Corona wrote.

At that event, Long stated a harsh truth about free-market housing: "If you are an income earner in our area, you can't afford a home in our area."

She explained that the area median income (AMI) for a three-person household in 2023 was $103,000 in Pitkin County and $89,000 in Garfield. Average individual salaries in 2023 were $76,000 in Pitkin County and $61,000 in Garfield County, according to data from labor market analytical firm Chmura. Even a household earning three times the AMI cannot afford the county's median free-market home price of $3 million in 2023, said Long.

"The issue of housing affordability in the valley has significantly worsened in recent years," reported the *Daily News*, quoting Long, who said, "The percentage of home sales affordable to a Pitkin County household at median wage decreased from 23% to 9% between 2015 and 2022. The same number dropped from 78% to 37% in Garfield County."

The picture for rental housing is similarly dire, according to Mary Coddington of Cappelli Consulting. Quoting a regional housing availability study contracted by West Mountain, Coddington said that "increased stock of affordable housing is essential to support working locals in the Roaring Fork Valley." However, high rents have put secure, long-term housing beyond the budgets of many workers who are spending more than 36% of their incomes on housing, which the Colorado Housing Finance Authority considers financially unhealthy.

"One of the appealing parts of this job is knowing how critical housing is," Long said. "When I was renting and my landlord was increasing my rent to a price that I couldn't afford, the daily stress of trying to figure out how I was going to stay in the community that I love with the sacrifices I'm going to need to make in order to afford it here only grew."

Long was faced with a profound choice: "Was I going to have to move and get a new job in a community I'm not familiar with and a place where I don't want to live, and to move my children? That daily stress affected me. And I can't imagine how that stress affects someone with even less means than I have. It affects your mental health and your physical health, your children's health, their stress, and your ability to help them with their homework. It is so foundational and has tentacles that touch everything if your housing is not stable and secure."

April Long, program director for West Mountain Regional Housing Coalition, is shown here in February 2024 outlining a proposed program to the Pitkin County Board of County Commissioners that would help homebuyers in the region.
JASON CHARME/ASPEN DAILY NEWS

NO-GROWTH AFFORDABLE HOUSING

RECENTLY RETIRED ATTORNEY DAVE MYLER founded what would become the West Mountain Regional Housing Coalition in 2018 with the late Bill Lamont, both as a humane gesture to working commuters and as a practical step toward addressing regional economic stability. The nonprofit coalition applies donated funds to subsidize and stabilize housing for qualified buyers who accept deed restrictions in order to keep affordable housing sustainable.

"The region is really one community connected by a very mobile workforce," said Myler. "That workforce is mobile because of Highway 82 and I-70. That's why it makes sense to take a regional approach to the housing problem like we did with transportation. We are one community. Do we have differences? Of course: political differences, economic differences, all kinds of differences. But we're basically one community connected by a workforce that drives up and down the valley every day."

Myler recalled a propitious meeting with Lamont, an influential and far-thinking community planner. "I was in City Market in Carbondale in 2018, and ran into Bill. He was standing in front of the Cheerios and said, 'We've got to do something about this housing problem in the valley.' We talked, had a meeting, did some thinking and agreed to form a regional, multi-jurisdictional housing authority made up of all the local governments in the valley that could raise taxes to pay for housing solutions. We didn't think at that time of going past Glenwood Springs, but that would come later."

Ideally, said Myler, the coalition would derive taxing power to raise funds for housing solutions. "Think of where we might be today," he mused, "if we had started taxing the billionaires of Pitkin County in 2018—or a decade earlier."

Although the idea of a regional special taxing district to fund housing proved politically untenable at that time, Myler and Lamont succeeded in bringing local governments to the table, fostering a collaboration that resulted in a landmark 2019 greater Roaring Fork Valley housing need assessment. In 2022, the West Mountain Regional Housing Coalition incorporated as a nonprofit. Today, its membership is made up of representatives from the city of Aspen, Pitkin County, Snowmass Village, Basalt, Carbondale, Eagle County, Glenwood Springs, Colorado Mountain College and RFTA. Myler serves as at-large director, with Long, program director, as the first hired staff. Each entity donated $10,000 for 2022-23, with more funds on the table this year. The coalition is also applying for grants.

Since growth and development are hot-button controversies throughout the region, the coalition is pursuing a buy-down program in which existing housing units are purchased, converted to affordable units and deed-restricted in order to maintain price control. "The program not only provides homes working residents can afford," Myler said. "It preserves workforce housing. Buy-downs make sense."

Long said the coalition aimed to officially launch the buy-down program in July 2024 as they continue work to secure funding. To date, Long said, the coalition has secured commitments from Carbondale ($100,000), Snowmass Village ($250,000) and Glenwood Springs ($200,000). In February, Pitkin County commissioners signaled support for contributing up to $2 million, but on May 28 lowered that commitment to $1 million for what Long has dubbed the "Good Deeds" program. The county's potential pledge was reduced in part based on discomfort some commissioners felt with spending county funds on housing purchases beyond their boundaries. The city of Aspen is considering a $450,000 contribution.

While that's a start, Myler noted that enough money to acquire a substantial volume of buy-downs remains a still-missing ingredient. "To make a serious difference," he said, "we need hundreds of millions." A coalition-initiated survey underwritten by the Colorado Housing and Finance Authority (CHFA), released in 2019 and reflecting pre-COVID-19 market conditions, revealed a 4,000-unit housing shortfall in the region, which included Gypsum.

"It means there are 4,000 individuals and households that are paying up to 70% of their income for housing and not the 30% that is an agreed-upon standard based on income," Myler said. "They are driving too far to get to and from work, and they are living in garages and substandard conditions."

Like Schwartz, Myler is a housing advocate veteran who began in 1979 as town counsel for Snowmass Village, where he advocated for worker-housing mitigation when the Creekside development was built. "I was sitting across the table from Jim Light and Jim Chaffin," Myler said of the Creekside development team, "and they were extremely supportive, and that piqued my interest."

Later, Myler was appointed to the APCHA board, then received an appointment to the CHFA board from then-Gov. Bill Ritter. "I learned a lot during that mission," said Myler, who was involved with numerous affordable housing projects.

"It's an obvious need," he said. "You can't have a healthy community with a workforce that's not content with where they live. It's just essential. The objective is to build healthy communities. Providing an adequate supply of affordable housing is a key ingredient in that. Everyone benefits—employers, employees and our guests."

Besides garnering the public support, the coalition aims to attract donations from practically and socially minded philanthropists who recognize housing buy-downs as a benefit to stabilizing workforce and

Recently retired attorney David Myler co-founded the nonprofit West Mountain Regional Housing Coalition in 2018, for which he serves as at-large director. The organization has brought local governments to the table to discuss housing as a regional issue. PAUL ANDERSEN/ASPEN JOURNALISM

community housing. That could include "anyone who wants Aspen to maintain its status as a world-class resort and a healthy community with someone who's smiling at you when you order a drink at the bar, with first responders and people at the hospital, with people who are teaching our kids, and more," Myler said. "In order to keep this, we need to house the workforce. Here's a chance to be part of the solution. Write us a check."

West Mountain Regional Housing Coalition is also working to develop a program it hopes to launch next year that would help renters cover the often crippling expense of coming up with a deposit plus first and last month's rent when signing a new lease. A recent survey of the rental market commissioned by the coalition found that "deed-restricted tenants showed greater satisfaction with their housing and landlord responsiveness. However, the survey also showed that Hispanic tenants were disproportionately absent from deed-restricted rental housing in the valley where benefits fall largely to white households."

BUILD BIG OR GO HOME

A PROFOUND TESTAMENT to disproportionality came from Aspen in March when two real estate sales records were broken in rapid succession. First was the sale price of a vacation house that topped $77 million. Just two weeks later, the ceiling was raised to $108 million in what mirrored a Boardwalk/Park Place property quest where the wealth spent on top-end housing is far in excess of anything measurable by normative standards within the regional housing sphere.

Evidence of this Grand Canyon-scale economic rift between the American aristocracy and the working class is nothing new. Thorstein Veblen coined the phrase "conspicuous consumption" in his 1899 book, *The Theory of the Leisure Class*, in which he lampooned wealthy elites for parading their material excesses as a self-inflating symbol of status.

"The motive that lies at the root of ownership is emulation," wrote Veblen. "The possession of wealth confers honor; it is an invidious distinction . . . where the possession of property becomes the basis of popular esteem. It also becomes a requisite to that complacency we call self-respect . . . The basis on which good repute in any highly organized industrial community ultimately rests is pecuniary strength; and the means of showing pecuniary strength and so of gaining and retaining a good name, are leisure and a conspicuous consumption of goods."

Visible displays of wealth have a long history that is reflected in today's local housing situation. During medieval times, "the wealthiest lived in impressive castles and had lots of people who worked for them," states investment blog Investopedia, "whilst the poorest worked on landowners' farms." If that sounds familiar, it is because Aspen's escalated housing market smacks of medievalism.

Veblen's more damning indictment is what he labeled "conspicuous waste" of both resources and human labor. To waste resources, one had only to exceed corporeal needs to feed insatiable appetites. Veblen deemed the wasting of a laborer's time on nonessential, status-building displays as the most odious use of pecuniary power.

The outrageous escalation of Aspen's housing prices and a willingness to spend it higher is attributable to the "Veblen Paradox," a phenomenon in which the demand for a product increases as its price increases, contradicting the typical laws of supply and demand. That someone would spend $108 million for a 22,000-square-foot mansion would have even made Veblen blush.

That record sale elicited the following description in the April 17 edition of the *Aspen Times*: "The 22,405-square-foot property includes 11 bedrooms and 17 bathrooms and sits on 4.5 acres in the coveted Red Mountain neighborhood of Aspen . . . making it the highest price residential sale ever in Aspen and the state of Colorado."

The *Times* offered a community perspective on the record-breaking sale, in which the buyer made the cash purchase for $4,820.35 per square foot: "The quality of life in Aspen is exceptional," one of the real estate brokers who had negotiated with the buyer and the seller was quoted as saying. "The real estate prices aren't high here just because of the really nice houses. It's because of the community, and it's because the city of Aspen is a really special place."

But a special place for how long? Habitat for Humanity's Schwartz warned of housing price disparity in a May newsletter, saying, "The ever-increasing cost of free-market housing is significantly diminishing the ability of our businesses, institutions and communities to function and deliver services."

WHAT WOULD JESUS DO?

THE NEW YORK TIMES wrote a striking headline for an April 27, 2024 story: "What Would Jesus Do? Tackle the Housing Crisis, Say Some Congregations." Empty pews in Inglewood First United Methodist Church of Inglewood, California, prompted the Rev. Victor Cyrus-Franklin to determine that housing prices were threatening his flock. This prompted support for the "Yes in God's Backyard" movement, which aims to build affordable housing on faith organizations' properties.

Reported the *Times*: "Inglewood First United Methodist is one of a growing number of churches, mosques and synagogues that have started developing low-cost housing on their properties. In interviews, faith leaders said they hoped to help with the growing housing and homeless problems that were most acute in California but have spread across the country. Virtually every major religious tradition teaches the importance of helping those in need: The idea fits the mission."

Some universities are also facing housing pressures, stated another *Times* headline from Dec. 18, 2023: "How College Football Is Clobbering Housing Markets Across the Country." Instead of a focus on God, it's all about football. The *Times* article described how "short-term rentals are taking over college towns, fueled by wealthy fans and investors who turn homes into hotels for a few weeks out of the year" and leave them to stand empty the rest of the year.

Providing accessible, affordable housing has become a matter of virtue for some community members and organizations that foster care for their citizens. That's why Schwartz has undertaken a nearly messianic mission to move the needle on accessible housing for people in the Aspen-to-Parachute region whose lives are deeply touched by Habitat for Humanity, as testimonials shared by the organization proclaim:

> Dear Friend of Habitat RFV,
>
> My name is Jessica, and I am the proud mom of my 3 1/2-year-old daughter and a new Habitat for Humanity homeowner! I am writing today to thank you for helping my family during an incredibly challenging time filled with so many struggles.
>
> My daughter is such a happy, outgoing little girl that has many struggles due to health concerns in her life. As a mother, it is incredibly difficult for me to continue residing in an old apartment complex that has continued to develop more and more issues that make me concerned for the health of my daughter and me. I have struggled daily worrying about my daughter's health and our safety that living in the apartments has brought to our lives.
>
> When I applied for a Habitat for Humanity affordable home in Wapiti Commons, I hoped and prayed that we would be blessed, and we were! I have met the other new homeowners and worked with the Habitat for Humanity build crew and Restore workers and felt from the start that this was a community of people that would benefit my daughter and myself by providing the family-type atmosphere we have craved! Being selected has allowed me to work alongside the experienced team of builders as our new home is built from the ground up.
>
> Thanks to you and your generosity, I am now a proud owner of a new, safe home for my daughter and me to grow together alongside an amazing new community of friends. I can proudly tell her that we are home and surrounded by safe people. I get to see the smile on her face as she grows up

happy and healthy with new friends close by. Our lives have been changed for the better, thanks to you!

Sincerely, Jessica

Consider the change of life in another Habitat for Humanity recipient as stated on the Habitat website:

Before buying a Habitat for Humanity home, Karla lived with her two small children in a concrete-floored garage, paying $850 monthly. Her daughter is 3 and her son is 12. They had a single bed, a toilet, a small sink, a small fridge and a single burner on which to cook. There were no windows to provide light, and temperature regulation was nonexistent.

Karla is a local banker and an essential, hard-working community member. As a single mother, Karla does everything she can to provide for her children. No mother wants to live in this situation, but, unfortunately, these are the housing options that were available for her to make ends meet. However, this is not where Karla's story ends! Karla has moved into her beautiful new townhome with three bedrooms and two bathrooms for her children to grow and flourish.

Jess Montour and daughter enjoy their new home at Habitat for Humanity's Wapiti Commons in Rifle where they took up residency in April 2024. Six families now reside in this affordable housing neighborhood.

HABITAT FOR HUMANITY

CHAPTER 10

Housing Challenges and Solutions

Housing innovations create community stability

THE REGIONAL HOUSING CRISIS is rife with both challenges and opportunities for communities from Aspen to Parachute. Perhaps the most optimistic sign is the growing awareness—socially, economically and politically—of how housing underscores community health, vitality and sustainability. This cohesive awareness is a critical step toward communities addressing a shared burden.

A stark reminder was reported in the Wednesday, June 5 *Aspen Times*, revealing that the Aspen School District's Moody's credit rating is taking a hit because of a low general fund reserve balance. A lack of affordable teacher housing also factored in: "The credit profile of Aspen School District is supported by Aspen's highly-affluent economy, anchored by world-renowned Aspen and Snowmass Ski Resorts," reported the *Times*, quoting a document from the rating agency. "Property value appreciation has accelerated in recent years due to strong demand in the area, including a 58% increase in assessed valuations for fiscal year 2024 to $5.5 billion. However, this economic strength and significant rise in property values presents challenges related to cost of living and housing affordability for district staff, which makes it more difficult for the district to attract and retain teachers, and subsequently increases the operating costs of the district."

Sydney Schalit, director of Manaus, stands with Brianda Cervantes, housing advocate for residents of 3-Mile Mobile Home Park on the south end of Glenwood Springs. PAUL ANDERSEN/ASPEN JOURNALISM

The housing issue has become a pressing concern throughout the region, where necessity becomes the mother of invention as seen in varied approaches to address a growing community crisis.

3-MILE PARK INSPIRES OWNERSHIP CONVERSION

IN 2014, Brianda Cervantes emigrated from Mexico, where she was born and raised. She came to the United States as a promising young woman with a law degree, first locating in Carbondale, then Glenwood Springs, where she has lived for a year working as a housing advocate for residents of 3-Mile Mobile Home Park, on the south end of Glenwood Springs.

"I came to Glenwood Springs for this opportunity," she said, "because, as a single mother with my son, housing stability means a lot to me. I wanted to help others through what I know from my own life experience, which I do with passion."

Cervantes sees her role as more than a job. She sees it as a mission for building community through an ownership conversion where residents of the 20-unit park have been renters, some for more than 30 years. Now, they are on a path to becoming owners through an innovative approach involving partnerships and subsidies.

"These are people who never imagined they could become owners," Cervantes said, "and now that we're involved, it has been a life-changing experience. This park can be theirs one day, their families are going to be stable, they don't have to worry about what's going to happen next, and that brings safety and comfort for them."

Housing security as a social-justice goal is the drive behind the 3-Mile conversion, thanks to Manaus Fund, a regional philanthropic nonprofit that advocates for community values in the Roaring Fork Valley. To make the conversion possible, Manaus allied with the Roaring Fork Community Development Corp. (RFCDC) to act as the financial entity that will ensure an affordable sale to the park owners.

"We knew that 3-Mile residents were interested in a self-purchase," said Sydney Schalit, director of Manaus. Too small for a traditional resident-occupied community (ROC) model, which requires 25 or more units and comes with financing from the state of Colorado, the 3-Mile Park conversion required that Manaus become the chief advocate and the RFCDC the financial backer, making a three-way partnership with park residents.

The first hurdle was cultivating a "friendly seller," meaning owners who would discount the price of the 14-acre site as a social good. Schalit said that Manaus intervened early in the process when it became clear that the children of long-time park owner Ben Krueger, who passed away in 2021, were prepared to sell. "They ended up becoming friendly sellers," Schalit said. RFCDC struck a deal to buy the park from the Kruegers for $2.4 million, and the sale closed in April 2023.

The park's decades-long residents were personally invested because their kids and now grandkids live there. This became a strong incentive for the conversion. Now that the process is underway, Manaus, which is planning to wind down its operations late in 2024, intends to spin off the RFCDC and set it up for success to operate independently, similar to several other nonprofits previously incubated by Manaus. To facilitate the handoff, Manaus will provide a final round of operational grant funding to the RFCDC and assist in the assembly of a skilled and dedicated board of directors to guide it through the transition and the successful completion of resident ownership.

Housing as a humanitarian need reflects the mission of Manaus, self-described as "a social justice nonprofit that works in partnership with others to help create sustainable solutions to issues that further equity within our communities using the principles of community organizing and co-design to invest in solutions designed for, with and by the most vulnerable communities."

The word "manaus" is Portuguese for "the meeting of waters," a metaphor for a beneficial social confluence as intended by its late founder, George Stranahan, who posited: "Traditional charity tends to be doing it to them or doing it for them. Manaus is building a model where we do it with them. The model is a conscious effort to build a partnership of equals."

Other Manaus incubations include The Savings Collaborative—formerly LaMedichi—which supports regional community members with opportunities for financial literacy and stability; The Third Street Center in Carbondale, which serves as a critical professional and cultural hub by housing nonprofits, artists and the community since its launch in 2010; Mountain Voices Project, which was launched in 2019 and is building civic leaders in the community and helping to hold public systems accountable; and the Confluence Early Childhood Education (CECE) Coalition project, which, since 2017, has been working to improve access to early care and education for all members of the Parachute-to-Aspen region. Manaus has also been a supporter of Aspen Journalism by providing seed funding in 2011, shortly after the organization launched.

During a walk in 3-Mile park with Schalit and Cervantes on a sunny April morning, there was a palpable spirit of hope and promise in the air, and also the rush of 3-Mile Creek, which flows through the park. And when a small flock of domestic chickens strutted across the commons, there was an added note of rural homespun independence in a place where park children walk to a nearby school, and where a mutual sense of neighborliness abides.

"They're really a beautiful community," Cervantes said. "They care for each other. They're willing to work together. It's a small community and everybody feels welcome when they come together. They ask how they can help each other. And that's inspiring."

Schalit, who was born in Conifer, Colorado, and grew up in southern Texas, has applied her unique blend of marketing entrepreneurship and Peace Corps-veteran values (she served in the African nation of Mali) to the park, home to 100 residents—30 of whom are children younger than 18 and about 10 of whom are seniors or are on disability.

"In the last year, we've had really significant involvement with the community in which Brianda has been very instrumental," Schalit said. "Bringing on Brianda was critical because she is Latina and is a bilingual and bicultural community organizer, which serves well in a park where 65% of families are Latino or Spanish speaking. She has had similar experiences to the residents as an immigrant who has had housing challenges in the valley and has a deep sense of community."

Commitment to community, said Cervantes, came from her grandfather in Mexico: "When I was 5 years old—because of my family situation—I was raised by my grandfather, and we had a really strong connection. He was the first person that I found with a beautiful heart toward his community. He never went to school, but he was a politician at heart, always caring for his community. He was responsible for his community having water and all the basic services required to live. He taught me how to do hard work. He has been my role model and an inspirational person for me. That's where my passion comes from because he had a vision for me to help communities.

"If I can impact my community and the people around me in a positive way, I will do it. When I came to the United States, I had to handle so many struggles. God put me in better positions than I had before, so now it's time for me to give back because I'm feeling so grateful to be in the position I'm in."

Habitat for Humanity of the Roaring Fork Valley President Gail Schwartz speaks during a ceremony marking the opening of the 27-unit Basalt Vista affordable housing development in 2022. ASPEN DAILY NEWS

Cervantes has a key role at 3-Mile Park, said Schalit. "She has helped residents form subcommittees to bring them into constructive decision-making and help them consider and frame how they are going to run the park with their own management opportunities and bank accounts," Schalit said. "Community meetings have agendas, and residents bring up issues. Meetings are always facilitated and always interpreted live with Convey Language Solutions, which has been a great partner to make sure we have language justice at every meeting. And it's never English focused; it's Spanish focused, where English speakers are on the headsets."

Schalit said the RFCDC's 3-Mile Park purchase was made possible with debt structured so that the first three years of payments cover only interest, which the individual space rents fully pay, plus a small amount added to pay down the principal. "We're going to try to buy down the cost of the park with some fancy lending opportunities for the residents," Schalit said, "because there are a lot of agencies interested in supporting the purchase by the residents and a nonprofit landlord, so we're really optimistic." Eventually, the park will be sold to the residents as a collective. Residents' rental payments will cover their collective debt, expenses and park improvements. Together, they will own, operate and manage the park.

A conversion such as 3-Mile's meets many crucial criteria for regional affordable housing: It serves existing residents of a target demographic. It does not represent new growth and exists in an advantageous location. It empowers resident owners to be independent and innovative. It leads toward improvements based on pride of ownership. Most of all, it ensures housing security for its residents.

NEIGHBORHOODS, CRITICAL WORKFORCE AND MODULAR HOMES

THE NONPROFIT HABITAT FOR HUMANITY of the Roaring Fork Valley is striving to build homes for $305 per square foot and sell them for $200 per square foot to meet an 80% of area median income level for teachers, nurses and other essential workers. According to Gail Schwartz, this is part of the organization's pledge to create a housing pool for workers without tying them to a particular job through employer-provided housing, which creates vulnerability for families or individuals.

"Affordable housing is part of our infrastructure," said Schwartz, "like building a bridge or a road—deed-restricted in perpetuity to be affordable. We have to stabilize housing. We visit every family we work with and witness the conditions in which they are living, the instability and stress they are under, and the dislocation. That's a problem, and yet we expect them to function as professionals."

Addressing existing housing, Habitat for Humanity is creating opportunities for older adults to downsize and stay in the community, ensuring housing diversity while freeing up housing stock that is appropriate for incoming workers with families. Toward that goal, the organization has built Americans with Disabilities Act-accessible, one-bed flex units in Rifle to support older adults so they can downsize and still own.

Seeing the need for an expansive affordable housing push, Habitat's Roaring Fork chapter broke from the nonprofit's traditional volunteer-driven, one-house-at-a-time model in 2018 when it began construction on the 27-home Basalt Vista development.

The first homeowners moved into the new neighborhood, on a sunny slope behind Basalt High School, in 2019, to great fanfare, and the project won the local chapter national recognition, as reported by Andrew Travers for Aspen Journalism in 2022. The experience spurred the local Habitat leadership to find even-larger-scale housing solutions and less-expensive construction than the $12.8 million Basalt undertaking.

Habitat tweaked the Basalt Vista model for the Wapiti Commons project in Rifle, which broke ground in March 2022, using a thriftier panel-built construction for a 20-unit development. The first homeowners moved in in February, and Habitat expected to wrap up construction before the end of 2024.

Karla Quintana with her son and daughter celebrated moving into their Wapiti Commons affordable housing townhome in February 2024. Wapiti is a 20-unit Habitat for Humanity neighborhood project in Rifle with 10 townhomes and 10 condominiums.
HABITAT FOR HUMANITY

"One local teacher of 12 years lived in a rental," Schwartz said. "When she had her second child, that child slept in the bathroom—in the bathtub. She bought a unit at Basalt Vista, and they are in for the long game."

And so is Habitat for Humanity, where energy and resource efficiency are development goals. "We build only net-zero homes," said Schwartz, who gave an example of a new Habitat for Humanity housing development where "homeowners are paying $14 per month for all utilities but water, with onsite solar and built-in efficiencies that are a perpetual benefit." Residents live in their own dwellings with minimal financial stress, Schwartz said. "Affordable mortgage. Affordable utilities. That's affordability!"

Residential consistency ensures housing security and manifests ideal possibilities, Schwartz said, adding, "We believe in ownership because that is how we stabilize the community. We all want the American dream, and for that, we need to have a bold vision and bold leaders."

She added that Habitat is putting in an offer to purchase a two-year-old 88-unit Glenwood Springs apartment building that was developed as free-market rentals. If the purchase is successful, Habitat will convert the units to condominiums and sell them with a deed restriction to local workers.

Jess and Kim Lawson (left) and their children stand before their new housing unit at Wapiti Commons, an affordable housing development built by Habitat for Humanity, where they moved in April 2024. HABITAT FOR HUMANITY

Schwartz urges local governments to raise the affordable housing bar for new development far above the region's average of 10% to 30% of new units required to be deed-restricted. "We need 70% affordable housing," she said, to ensure housing for essential services such as "education, health care, emergency services and transportation—all of which suffer without housing. What happens when you need an ambulance in Aspen and the driver lives in New Castle? Have you tried to call a plumber lately?"

Dave Myler of West Mountain Regional Housing Coalition ups the ante even higher: "I'd like to see new developments have 80% affordable housing, not the 20% we're getting now. We don't need more second homes. We need affordable housing."

No single solution is going to resolve the housing problem, said Schwartz, who advocates a triple front that establishes housing as the top priority for regional nonprofit support. "There are three solutions: bold leadership, philanthropic engagement and public/private partnerships," she said. "Sure, it's nice to have museums and culture, but every one of those nonprofits needs to house their employees. Who do they call? Habitat."

In addition to building homes, the organization is in the process of constructing a modular housing plant in Rifle on 10 acres where a team of trained workers can build upward of 100 homes each year, while training 100 students per year in advanced manufacturing. This $12.8 million net-zero production and education facility, expected to break ground in late 2024, could be transformational for this region. Specifically, Habitat for Humanity said, "This facility will contribute to the region's economic development and is projected to have 27 full-time employees. It is designed to diversify the workforce and economy for careers of the future."

"When you train an advanced manufacturing workforce in the Colorado River Valley, you attract new investment and create jobs there," Schwartz said. "And good luck to the resort communities when we have jobs for these young professionals to work in the communities where they live. This is a game changer because we're taking it to scale. We have a workforce deficit, and we are moving ahead."

Meanwhile, at Habitat for Humanity's Restore, a 40,000-square-foot warehouse outside Glenwood Springs, 30 employees assist customers in repurposing 3,000 tons of homebuilding goods a year—windows, doors, furniture—in another move toward housing affordability.

INSATIABLE HOUSING DEMAND

"JOBS ARE PLENTIFUL and employees are in demand throughout the Roaring Fork Valley," Schwartz wrote in a May newsletter to Habitat for Humanity supporters. "The 2019 housing study showed that our region, from Aspen to Parachute, would require 5,700 new homes for existing workforce families by 2027."

Although scalable action on workforce and community housing is underway in some sectors, the housing need mounts, with no peak in sight. A January 2024 housing forum at Willits was a "coming out" event for West Mountain Regional Housing Coalition nonprofit and yet was headlined in the *Aspen Daily News* as a "grim picture."

Aspen Daily News staff writer Austin Corona wrote: "Presenters at the event said West Mountain's debut is arriving at a time when affordable free-market housing is practically unattainable for local workers in many parts of the Roaring Fork Valley." Forum participant Mary Coddington of Cappelli Consulting said that "more than 2,000 housing units are currently planned or in development in the Roaring Fork Valley area, though more than half will be listed or rented at market rate," implying their unavailability to workers, who have the greatest need.

To support greater housing availability in the area and to defray the stigma that affordable housing is a growth generator, West Mountain board member and Pitkin County community resilience manager Ashley Perl said that "rather than constructing new units, the coalition is seeking 'development-neutral' approaches." Perl offered details of three pilot programs that the coalition plans to roll out.

In one program, West Mountain would fund households' first- and last-month rent payments to help with signing new leases. These payments, which are often rolled up with other costs into an initial deposit, can sometimes add up to about $10,000 for a single household. In another program, West Mountain plans to financially incentivize homeowners throughout the region to build additional dwelling units on their properties and rent them as deed-restricted housing. West Mountain's largest program will be a "deed-restriction program" or "buy-down program," in which the coalition will partially subsidize purchases of existing homes for working locals in the Roaring Fork and Colorado River valleys with the condition that buyers place their homes under deed-restrictions to ensure long-term affordability.

To fund these programs, the coalition hopes to bring in donations from private citizens and employers as well as contributions from member organizations and regional governments. West Mountain founder Myler said the coalition has already received contributions between $100,000 and $1 million from local governments and organizations for the deed-restriction program in 2024, and that millions more would be needed to make a dent.

"It takes everybody working together to create a package that helps with this problem," West Mountain program director April Long said at the close of the forum.

On Feb. 21, 2024 Snowmass Village Town Council approved a sketch plan for 80 new affordable workforce housing units on a site above Town Hall—one of the largest projects for workforce housing coming from the town's 2021 housing master plan. The proposed development would split 80 units between two buildings up to 78 feet tall, with a shared parking garage between the buildings. Some Town Council members had expressed concern about the project in past meetings, citing the size of the two buildings and the steepness of the land, but in the end, they agreed it was important to pursue workforce housing development.

The Confluence is a six-unt affordable housing development being built on city-owned land by Habitat for Humanity at Eighth Street and Midland Avenue in Glenwood Springs. RICH ALLEN/ASPEN DAILY NEWS

Snowmass Village housing director Betsy Crum said 261 people are on the town's waitlist for affordable rentals; people can wait years before units become available; and the lack of affordable housing is burdening local businesses. In a survey conducted by the town in December 2023, 90% of local businesses that responded said difficulty with staffing was an issue, and 100% of those businesses said workforce housing assistance was the best way for the town to support their staffing challenges.

"We've had Taster's there since '01," Heather Huber, owner of Taster's Pizza and the Daly Diner, told Town Council, "and we've never had such a hard time finding housing for staff. We've debated having to close or having to shut down because there's simply no place for people to live."

Coincidentally, in February 2024, the Glenwood Springs *Post Independent* reported completion of the first units at Wapiti Commons in Rifle, a Habitat for Humanity project built on land donated in 2020 by regional developers Clay Crossland and Paul Adams. A celebration included a ceremony of presenting keys of their newly built homes to chosen families and a pledge to keep the momentum going.

A few weeks later, the *Post Independent* reported another affordable project in the works for Glenwood Springs. The Confluence housing development, at Eighth Street and Midland Avenue, grew out of two city-owned properties offered to bid. One site, on Airport Road, was dropped because of complications from residue from historic coke ovens. The Confluence was chosen and is underway for development by Habitat for Humanity in partnership with the city of Glenwood Springs. The current plan, which drew considerable input from an adjacent 100-home neighborhood, targets Glenwood Springs residents with at least two years of work history and incomes of 80% the area median. The development, approved and in process, entails six net-zero, deed-restricted condominium units.

"We really wanted to maintain the livability of the site and our commitments around the development," Schwartz said. "These will be beautiful homes."

Schwartz said Habitat for Humanity is still in the process of solidifying the project's overall cost. She expects, at a minimum, $1 million needed in subsidies. "And that is where we're going to come back to the community and ask for support," she said.

In the past couple of years, construction costs have gone up 37%, the impacts of which Schwartz said they've seen while building 20 homes in Rifle. "We're foreseeing a little bit of suffering for some of those costs," she said.

NOT IN MY BACKYARD

SENTIMENTS ON NEW HOUSING construction have become conflicted where neighborhood objections to development proposals have begun to overshadow affordable housing benefits. Resistance often comes from the unlikely source of working-class neighborhoods that are adjacent to parcels where it's still deemed affordable to build.

A Glenwood Springs project known as 480 Donegan was put forth by R2 Partners to annex West Glenwood property into the city and build 40 townhomes and 230 apartments, a small percentage of which was designated affordable. The project was approved by City Council in 2021, but it was overturned in a referendum brought by residents in an April 2022 special election. After the annexation and development were shot down by voters, the property owners switched their plan to storage and commercial development, which won approval and is currently underway.

"It is important to know that 75% of Glenwood employees commute in," said Schwartz. "The hospital and schools are in desperate need of employees."

Another potential housing development, Flying M, was voted down by the Garfield County Board of County Commissioners on Nov. 15, 2023. The project had proposed 146 two-story market-rate rental townhomes; 12 townhomes exclusively available to Roaring Fork School District employees; 10 accessory dwelling units (ADUs) in the commercial district; eight home sites with ADUs in a single-family residential zone; 12 deed-restricted affordable rental townhome units; and a 12-bed hospice home with two worker dwelling units.

"We're being pushed really hard for more housing in this county," Commissioner Tom Jankovsky said in the *Post Independent*. He supported the project with this caveat: "Traffic and loss of rural character are real issues, but I think the housing benefits outweigh the deficits."

His opinion was not shared by soon-to-retire and long-standing Commissioner John Martin, who said, "Have we lost our rural character? Absolutely, and we lost it a long time ago. We've lost that rural character in Glenwood Springs. We are now Breckenridge or Aurora. I see the same buildings in Aurora as I do in Glenwood Springs, and I don't want to see that anymore. I know I'm hanging on to the past, and that has been my nature: to try to stabilize the community and really make the right choices."

For Commissioner Mike Samson, his "no" vote was predicated on public sentiment: "All the people who are from that area that spoke today are adamantly opposed to this designed project, and that carries a lot of weight with me because those are the neighbors. That's their neighborhood, and they're concerned about it." The board denied the application, 2-1.

In April 2024, Glenwood Springs voters amplified their concerns on growth and upped their political power over development in a landmark plebiscite known as Ballot Question A, which passed with 78% approval. The *Aspen Daily News* reported that the measure "added language to the city's home rule charter that any annexation of land or any residential/mixed-use housing on city-owned land will, after approval from the city, go to a public vote. Additionally, any development permit adding more than four new dwellings will be subject to review by the planning and zoning commission and approval of City Council. Previously, developments of more than eight units required planning and zoning review, and more than 24 units required council approval."

The ballot question was introduced by Glenwood Springs resident Jon Banks under the banner of the "Keep Glenwood Glenwood" campaign. Banks gathered more than 800 signatures. "We've seen often that the council goes in one direction and the people go in a different one," Banks told the *Aspen Daily News*. Support for Ballot Question A was garnered from residents who believe that the Glenwood Springs City Council "had not focused enough on quality of life for its current residents," reported the *Daily News*.

For Clark Anderson, a community organizer who heads Community Builders, a Glenwood Springs nonprofit, the new legislation adds yet another obstacle to addressing the regional housing crisis.

"I really believe it's going to make a lot of the challenges we're facing here worse," Anderson said in the *Daily News*. "And it's going to change the character of the community a lot in terms of its accessibility for workaday folks who I always have thought have been such a great part of the backbone of this community."

Statewide, housing is a foremost concern, stated Colorado Gov. Jared Polis during a regional "State of the State" address he delivered at Colorado Mountain College in Glenwood Springs on Jan. 29, 2024. Polis' visit was foreshadowed by a news release stating that "housing topped the list of Colorado's 'great challenges.'"

"The good news is that people want to live in Colorado," said Polis in an *Aspen Daily News* report, "but the bad news is the word has gotten out. And that's driven up home prices." Polis' observation was followed by a pledge to explore "innovative housing opportunities," which Polis did with a brief visit to the Valley Alliance to End Homelessness in Glenwood Springs, tour of a pilot modular housing initiative in Eagle and a look at an accessory dwelling unit in Glenwood Springs owned by Glenwood Springs City Council member Jonathan Godes.

In his speech, Polis said that "artificial constraints" on housing supply are preventing Colorado from meeting its housing demand and that "workers are being forced to move farther from where they work in order to find affordable housing, meaning that in a single year, the average Coloradan now spends $1,800 per year in gas for their commutes. The answer to affordability," Polis said in the *Daily News* report, "is not to make people live further and further away."

A pressing issue mentioned to Polis during his visit with Valley Alliance to End Homelessness is securing housing for the 70 Venezuelan refugees who found shelter under the Highway 133 bridge outside Carbondale in January 2024. It was reported that more Venezuelan immigrants have arrived in other cities across Colorado, including more than 26,000 in Denver.

Chickens have free range at 3-Mile Mobile Home Park thanks to the city of Glenwood Springs allowing poultry raising in certain areas within its urban boundaries.
PAUL ANDERSEN/ASPEN JOURNALISM

The *Daily News* reported that "VAEH has hired two new 'housing navigators' whose job will be to communicate with local landlords about making their properties part of the VAEH system.

Jose Saez, one of the new housing navigators, said he will look high and low to find viable options. 'I'll knock on the door and I'll ask your friends, I'll ask your friends' friends, and I'll ask your friend's dog, just to try to help somebody get housing.'"

"Without supply, we are losing our workforce, and this was just validated by the state of Colorado demographer," said Kathleen Wanatowicz, a consultant who has worked on numerous housing and infrastructure projects. Referencing March data from the Colorado Department of Local Affairs, she said that data reveals that the regional labor force will be tighter and that it will be harder to compete for the best and the brightest, that people 65 and older represent the fastest-growing demographic in Garfield County, which strains goods and services, and that people are aging in place in Colorado, limiting housing turnover needed for a new generation of working-class residents.

WHERE AFFORDABLE HOUSING COLLIDES WITH GROWTH

BUILDING NEW AFFORDABLE HOUSING is no mean feat, especially in a region where real estate is sky high, construction costs are through the roof and housing developments have become spurs for community pushback.

Real estate and construction costs can be subsidized, but political will is a cultural hurdle that thwarts the best of intentions. Glenwood Springs' Ballot Question A puts up a wall to new development, and yet attests that local control of community culture is a democratic mainstay.

Schwartz has had to answer to complaints about growth, which she said are based on a misunderstanding. "People say, 'Oh, they're just growing the community.' No, no, no!," Schwartz said. "We're just taking those people that are already part of the community and stabilizing them."

The goal of a project such as Habitat for Humanity's The Confluence isn't to bring new people into Glenwood Springs, Schwartz said, but to provide homes for those who are already living and working in the city limits.

"Our goal is to create secure homes for people to live and work in Glenwood," Schwartz said. "Is that going to be a firefighter or a teacher or a RFTA employee? We're taking people from a rental unit into a permanent home so they can continue to participate in the community and give back to the community, shop in the community, etc. When people receive these homes, they stay and continue working in the community. There is a continual drumbeat by business owners, the institutions, the hospitals and RFTA, saying, 'We need housing.' That is one voice. The [Glenwood Springs] government, in their openness and willingness to support affordable housing, is another voice."

As Habitat for Humanity is mandated to serve existing residents at The Confluence, the 3-Mile Mobile Home Park represents an ownership conversion that is making owners out of renters, with no new growth. Meanwhile, West Mountain Regional Housing Coalition is providing creative options through conversions of existing housing stock where new growth is defrayed by deed restricting existing units.

"We are not building housing," Long said at an Aspen Journalism-hosted housing forum in Carbondale in December, "but are looking to buy down existing housing and resell with price caps and deed restrictions. We also offer rental assistance—first and last—to get people in homes."

Michael Kinsley is a former Pitkin County commissioner who served on the board from 1975 to 1985. He was instrumental in initiating a countywide affordable housing strategy that later grew into the Aspen Pitkin County Housing Authority (APCHA). MICHAEL KINSLEY

Pitkin County commissioners on May 28, 2024 agreed to $1 million in support of the West Mountain buy-down program. With these funds, the coalition's buy-down program will be offered to buyers who find free-market homes for their full-time, primary residence with purchase-price caps of $1.5 million in Pitkin County and Basalt; $1.2 million in the Roaring Fork portion of Garfield County, including Glenwood Springs; and $800,000 in western Garfield County. The Roaring Fork portion of Eagle County would fall under a similar buy-down program offered by Eagle County government.

"West Mountain would provide up to 30% of the contracted purchase price in exchange for the buyer placing a deed-restriction on the property," reported the *Daily News*, after which Long remarked: "This brings down the total amount required from the buyer and bridges the gap between what is available on the market and what is affordable." Further, the deed restriction would limit appreciation of a subsidized residence to 3% annually. There would be no income cap on buyers, but they couldn't own other residential property in the region or anywhere else.

"I think we need to be a leader in the valley," said Commissioner Steve Child in support for the donation, "and this is our opportunity to step up."

AN APPROPRIATE HOUSING MIX AND WELL-BEING

FORMER PITKIN COUNTY COMMISSIONER Michael Kinsley served on the board from 1975 to 1985 and was instrumental in initiating a countywide affordable housing strategy that later grew into the Aspen-Pitkin County Housing Authority (APCHA).

Admitting to a "heretical" view—given that he was a commissioner when the county commissioners radically downzoned much of the county in the 1970s and given that he currently serves on the Pitkin County Open Space and Trails Board—Kinsley suggested a radical new look at key open space parcels that could rank highest for workforce housing such as half the Aspen municipal golf course and a portion of the Marolt Open Space.

Suggesting a nuanced approach to building new affordable housing based on a mix of pragmatics and ideology, Kinsley said, "Adding housing supply will not reduce prices in a highly inflated economy. Second-homeowners and retirees will always be able to outbid local working people. Economists call it an inelastic demand, which changes the balance of supply and demand. This implies that there is a significant role for nonprofits, development corporations and local government to solve the problem."

The first order of business, if significant progress is to be made, said Kinsley, "is to ignore governmental, jurisdictional boundaries, which just get in the way of solving these regional problems. I say this having been a county commissioner."

Kinsley recommends taking an inventory of all possible sites with evaluations for appropriateness based on aesthetics; biodiversity; proximity to employment or public transit; neighborhood impact; public cost of services and infrastructure; traffic; effects on employees; and other considerations.

"Any new affordable development will incite NIMBY-oriented opposition, for which there are valid reasons," he said. "However, objective criteria would overrule the NIMBY approach."

He also sounded a pragmatic note regarding immigration. "Regardless of what you think about the immigrant issue, our economy needs them in very practicable ways," he said. "Is the tourist economy here headed for a significant failure due to the unavailability of working people? I keep hearing about huge employee shortages in all kinds of businesses. So, this is not about cultural empathy, but hard-edged economics. There is a need for working people and for a viable way for them to come to work."

Housing directly impacts the economic viability of the upvalley resorts, he said, as traditional cohorts are no longer available to clean rooms and tend grounds, "and that even includes lawyers and doctors. We probably don't need more lawyers," quipped Kinsley, "but we'll always need more medical professionals."

Kinsley disagrees with the "messy vitality" planning notion of integrating workers across cultural townscapes, questioning the practicality of mixing tourist/second-home densities with employee densities. "There are not the places to do this," he said. "What is pejoratively referred to as a ghetto is by definition a cohesive neighborhood or community. That's the most comforting setting for the working population to live in—more like a real place."

Kinsley said Aspen is no longer suitable, despite its past intent, for integrating its diverse social strata. "There is now a group of people in Aspen who see community differently, not as a scrappy, funky place where working people and weird characters live," he said. "They see it as something more like a country club. Rather than assign a value judgment to that, it's important to recognize that a country club needs maids and groundskeepers. The local economy requires that we have those workers to operate the economy."

The housing challenge is interwoven throughout our diverse regional fabric, from Aspen to Parachute. It touches all walks of life and all manners of lifestyle. Housing is fundamental to American psychologist Abraham Maslow's hierarchy of needs, where belonging to a community through family and friends is crucially important. "Housing is one of the most important social determinants of health," *Time* magazine quoted "Legacy" author and Advancing Health Equity founder and CEO Uche Blackstock in its May 13 issue on health.

Although self-actualization stands at the peak of Maslow's pyramid, housing provides the necessary foundation for overall community health. Without firm foundations in housing, local and regional communities become unstable and unsustainable. Housing security is essential to who and what we are as a community.

HOUSING NON-PROFITS AND GOVERNMENT AGENCIES

Aspen Community Foundation
www.aspencommunityfoundation.org
Aspen Family Connections | www.aspenfamilyconnections.org
Aspen/Pitkin County Housing Authority (APCHA) | www.apcha.org
Colorado Housing and Finance Authority (CHFA)
www.chfainfo.com
Colorado River Valley Economic Development Partnership (CRVEDP)
www.edcconline.org
Community Builders | www.communitybuilders.org
Confluence Early Childhood Education (CECE)
www.cececoalition.org
Food Bank of the Rockies | www.foodbankrockies.org
Habitat for Humanity of the Roaring Fork Valley
www.habitatroaringfork.org
Harvest for Hunger | www.harvestforhungerco.org
Hurst Initiative at the Aspen Institute | www.aspen2parachute.org
Kind Neighbor Project
www.snowmasschapel.org/ministries/kind-neighbor-project
Lift-Up | www.liftup.org
Mountain Voices Project | www.mountainvoicesproject.org
Rifle Area Mountain Bike Organization (RAMBO)
www.riderifle.com
Roaring Fork Community Development Corp. (RFCDC)
www.roaringforkcdc.org
Roaring Fork Transportation Authority (RFTA) | www.rfta.com
Savings Collaborative | www.savingscollaborative.org
Valley Alliance to End Homelessness (VAEH)
www.westmountainhealthalliance.org
West Mountain Regional Housing Coalition | www.wmrhousing.org

ABOUT THE AUTHOR

PAUL ANDERSEN has been a professional writer for more than 45 years. His writing has earned him credits as a television scriptwriter, book author, screen writer, historian, magazine contributor, and columnist and contributing editor for the *Aspen Times*. He wrote a weekly opinion column, *Fair Game,* for over 30 years, for which he has won awards from the Colorado Press Association, and he is one of the longest continually published writers in the history of the *Aspen Times* over the course of four decades.

Andersen has published hundreds of newspaper articles, magazine features, authored fifteen books, written dozens of television scripts, and co-wrote the screen story for *China: The Panda Adventure* for IMAX Films (2000). His book, *The High Road to Aspen*, written in collaboration with photographer David Hiser, won the Colorado Book Award's Gold Medal in June 2015.

Andersen's journalistic career began in 1977 as reporter for the *Gunnison Country Times*. In 1980, he became a reporter/editor for the *Crested Butte Chronicle*, where he reported on all aspects of Gunnison County. In 1984, he joined the editorial staff of the *Aspen Times* and covered Aspen thoroughly and joyfully.

In 2005, Andersen partnered with the Aspen Institute to create *Nature & Society,* an executive seminar that immersed participants in wilderness while exploring philosophical, literary and historical perspectives on man and nature.

In 2013, Andersen founded the non-profit Huts For Vets, which he designed to help US military veterans plagued by trauma and other psychological challenges find peace and healing in the wilderness at the 10th Mountain Huts of Aspen.

Today, Andersen leads wilderness hikes for the Aspen Institute where he moderates the Great Books seminars. He enjoys reading philosophy and literature, and he hikes, skis and bikes the mountains and deserts of the American West. Bicycle tours have led him across Europe and Eurasia.

Andersen lives outside Basalt, up the Frying Pan Valley, 25 miles from Aspen, with his psychotherapist wife, Lu Krueger-Andersen. Their 30-year-old son, Tait, lives in Basalt with his wife Sarah and their new baby boy, Axel Andersen, named for Paul's Danish immigrant grandfather.

www.ingramcontent.com/pod-product-compliance
Lightning Source LLC
Chambersburg PA
CBHW060551030426
42337CB00021B/4536